Tics and Tourette Syndrome

Tics and Tourette Syndrome
A Handbook for Parents and Professionals

Uttom Chowdhury

Foreword by Isobel Heyman

Jessica Kingsley Publishers
London and Philadelphia

First published in the United Kingdom in 2004
by Jessica Kingsley Publishers
116 Pentonville Road
London N1 9JB, UK
and
400 Market Street, Suite 400
Philadelphia, PA 19106, USA

www.jkp.com

Library of Congress Cataloging in Publication Data
Chowdhury, Uttom, 1967-
    Tics and Tourette syndrome : a handbook for parents and professionals / Uttom
Chowdhury ; foreword by Isobel Heyman.-- 1st American pbk. ed.
    p. cm.
    Includes bibliographical references and index.
    ISBN 1-84310-203-X (pbk.)
    1. Tourette syndrome in children--Popular works. 2. Tic disorders--Popular works. I.
Title.
    RJ496.T68C47 2004
    618.92'83--dc22

                                    2004006405

British Library Cataloguing in Publication Data
A CIP catalogue record for this book is available from the British Library

ISBN-13: 978 1 84310 203 8
ISBN-10: 1 84310 203 X

Printed and Bound in Great Britain by
Athenaeum Press, Gateshead, Tyne and Wear

For my wife, Ruth, and son, Sacha

Contents

List of tables

Foreword

Tourette Syndrome fascinates neurologists and psychiatrists. The unusual symptoms and behaviours, including the involuntary movements and noises which characterize this condition, have inspired scholarly descriptions and neuroscience investigations. But Tourette Syndrome is much more than 'interesting cases' for the textbook or the research paper. This book delivers a practical and timely reminder that people with Tourette Syndrome lead ordinary lives but struggle with their own and others' misunderstanding of the condition. Motor and vocal tics can be the least of the problem; children and adults often face the challenges of mental health problems and behavioural difficulties, as well as problems with friendships, education and employment.

In this much needed handbook, Dr Chowdhury reminds us that people with Tourette Syndrome and their families, friends and teachers need to understand and live with the condition. His starting point is not the huge body of scientific research on Tourette Syndrome, but rather the families themselves. This book is both unusual and refreshing in acknowledging that the parents of a child with Tourette's are the real experts. Improving knowledge and acquiring skills for helping the child is as much about professionals learning from parents as vice-versa. Dr Chowdhury has distilled into practical advice, the range of experiences and suggestions he has gathered from the many families he has worked with over the years.

This approach has produced a book with immediacy and warmth that every parent and carer will find useful. Dr Chowdhury has really listened to parents and integrated their messages into a concise and authoritative review of the current Tourette Syndrome literature. If the professionals who use this book can also learn from these parents, their patients with Tourette's will benefit tremendously.

Dr Chowdhury fills every page with clear, unsentimental yet sensitive advice. He reminds parents of skills they already have, but perhaps have forgotten to use. The child with Tourettes's may be overwhelming and frustrating at times, but reminding parents that much of this troublesome behaviour is ordinary, and just arrives in unpredictable ways, or in excessive amounts, can help make things manageable. Tourette Syndrome is a disorder that has always mystified, but Dr Chowdhury demystifies in a way that empowers. There are excellent tips on coping with a child who could be seen as more boisterous than average, moving on to how to deal with disruptive behaviour and rage. By helping parents to regain control, Dr Chowdhury is then able to helpfully raise issues of parents dealing with their own anger and frustration, a task which is impossible if parents wrongly feel blame or guilt.

The science of Tourette Syndrome is not neglected in the book and indeed families are amongst the first to campaign for more research into understanding the links between brain functioning and behaviour. Readers will find up-to-date summaries of current brain scanning and genetic research, drug treatments, and other research studies, written in a way that is accessible and informative. For children and families to become their own experts, they need to understand something of the underlying science, and the messages from recent research.

Tourette Syndrome can be distressing, troublesome and disabling, but whilst acknowledging the stresses, this handbook helps everyone to see the positives and to deal with the difficulties. Dr Chowdhury reminds families that as well as seeking help, taking responsibility and becoming skilled and knowledgeable in the management of their child is half the battle. He reminds us that every individual with Tourette's has great potential, and indeed people with Tourette's in all walks of life, including sportsmen, actors, scientists to pick just a few examples, live happy and successful lives.

This book will be a valuable resource for my clinic at Great Ormond Street, and I know that parents and teachers, as well as general and specialist clinicians will all find it useful. I imagine that some young people will also dip into it, and perhaps use it as a way to discuss Tourette's with their friends or relatives. This book helps remove stigma, delivers clear, accurate information, abolishes misconceptions and gives proven, practical advice. This is just what is needed to help us to see Tourette's, not as a weird and rare condition, but as one affecting many young people who need understanding and advocacy.

Isobel Heyman
Consultant Child and Adolescent Psychiatrist and Lead Clinician
Tourette Syndrome Clinic
Great Ormond Street Hospital for Children

Acknowledgements

I would like to thank Professor Bryan Lask and Dr Jane Collins for inviting me to co-facilitate the parents' group at the Tic Disorders Clinic at Great Ormond Street Hospital, London, back in 1997 and for introducing me to the world of Tourette Syndrome.

I would like to thank my co-facilitator, Ms Susan Brown, for her words of wisdom and general advice when running the various groups and workshops.

I would like to thank Professor Mary Robertson for her encouragement, enthusiasm and help with research in Tourette Syndrome.

I would like to thank Dr Ruth Allen, Ms Rebecca Chilvers, Mrs Pene Sinnott, Dr Samuel Stein and several parents of children attending the Dunstable Child and Family Clinic, Bedfordshire, for reading and commenting on various chapter drafts.

Most of all I would like to thank all the parents with whom I have worked in various groups over the last few years. These parents have taught me more about tics and Tourette Syndrome than any book or series of lectures possibly could.

Preface

A few years ago, a colleague introduced me to a well-respected professor of adult psychiatry at a well-known institution in London. I was introduced as 'a clinician who has an interest in Tourette Syndrome'. Hearing this, the professor commented, 'I have been a psychiatrist for nearly 20 years and I have never seen a patient swear in my clinic.' Both my colleague and I were slightly surprised at this comment. Did this professor really think that Tourette Syndrome was all about people who swear? I did my best to explain to him that this was not the case but I am not sure if I convinced him. It made me think that if professors think like this, then we have got a long way to go with educating the public about this condition. However, if I am being totally honest, I probably used to think like this before I started seeing children with Tourette Syndrome. My previous knowledge of Tourette Syndrome was minimal and based on a page in a medical textbook and exaggerated portrayals in the media. I also cannot recall a single lecture on this condition at medical school (I think I went to most lectures!). Even today, the condition is only taught to medical students if there is a doctor affiliated to the medical school who just so happens to have an interest in tics.

My interest in Tourette Syndrome began in 1997 when I was invited to co-facilitate a parents' group for children with Tourette Syndrome. As I sat in this group, I was struck by what families had to put up with and the way families coped with the difficulties. It was clear that many of the professionals that the parents dealt with either had no knowledge of the condition or had incorrect information about it. Parents said that they could generally cope with the tics but it was dealing with relatives and members of the public that was probably the most challenging and painful aspect of this condition. Numerous examples were provided of incidents involving the public and professionals misunderstanding the children's condition. However, the group was not just a forum for talking about the difficulties of living with a child with Tourette Syndrome. Parents also shared amusing anecdotes and stories (it always impresses me how families use humour in the face of adversity).

As the months went by, I began to learn more and more about Tourette Syndrome. I started to see the condition in a new light and also hear about the effect it has on the family. Several issues came up time and time again. These were coping with bullying, behaviour management and dealing with schools. I went back to the medical textbooks to read about these issues but there was little information out there. Parents had said the same when researching for information.

In the group, parents were able to support each other and give advice and tips. When each group session finished, I started to make notes of comments that were said and the main issues discussed.

This book contains some of the information that was shared between parents as well as general advice on dealing with schools and behaviour management. I have also included chapters on self-esteem, anger management and bullying which I believe are relevant for many children with Tourette

Syndrome. These issues are rarely addressed in books and clinics, yet dealing with them can have a major impact in helping children cope with this condition. The book is intended for professionals as well as parents and I have tried to keep the medical jargon to a minimum.

I hope that the book will help the reader get a better understanding of the complexities of the condition, the associated difficulties, and the problems these children may face at school. I hope it also makes parents feel more empowered and able to cope with their child's diagnosis.

Ultimately, I hope that this book will at least contribute in some small way to making school days and home life more comfortable for the child who has Tourette Syndrome.

Uttom Chowdhury, 2004

Note

To avoid unnecessary repetition and for ease of reading, I have used the male gender throughout the book to represent the child with Tourette Syndrome.

CHAPTER ONE

What is Tourette Syndrome?

Introduction

The first description of someone with Tourette Syndrome in the medical literature was by Itard, in 1825, who wrote about a woman, the Marquise de Dampierre, who was severely affected by motor and vocal tics. Sixty years later, in 1885, a French physician, Georges Gilles de la Tourette, described nine patients with childhood-onset tics, who made uncontrollable noises and utterances (Robertson 2000). The condition was thought to be rare and clinicians assumed that the causes were psychological in origin, despite Gilles de la Tourette originally suggesting the condition was heritable. This all changed in the 1960s with the recognition of the beneficial effects of certain drugs on the symptoms. This then led on to much research into the condition, particularly in the 1980s and 1990s, and it is now recognized as a biological, genetic disorder with a spectrum of behavioural symptoms.

What is a tic?

A tic is an involuntary, rapid, recurrent, non-rhythmic motor or vocal action. It is sudden and purposeless. Tics consist of simple or coordinated, repetitive or sequential, movements, gestures and utterances that mimic fragments of normal behaviour. For descriptive purposes, they can be divided into simple or complex tics.

Simple motor tics are fast and meaningless and include eye blinking, grimacing and shoulder shrugging; while complex motor tics tend to be slower and may appear purposeful, e.g. hopping, kissing, touching objects, echopraxia (imitating movements of other people) and copropraxia (obscene gestures). (See Table 1.1)

Table 1.1 Examples of motor tics

Simple motor tics	Complex motor tics
Eye blinking	Hopping
Eye rolling	Jumping
Facial grimacing	Touching objects
Nose twitching	Twirling
Lip pouting	Gyrating
Shoulder shrugging	Bending
Arm jerking	Biting lip
Head jerking	Head banging
Head nodding	Kissing
Abdominal tensing	Licking
Kicking	Pinching
Finger movements	Facial gestures
Mouth opening	Copropraxia
Tongue protrusion	Echopraxia
Jaw snapping	
Teeth clicking	
Frowning	
Knuckle cracking	
Rapid jerking of any part of body	

Simple vocal tics include coughing, barking, clearing one's throat and whistling, whilst complex vocal tics include repeating certain words or phrases such as 'oh boy' or 'all right' or repeating a phrase until it sounds 'just right'. (See Table 1.2.)

| Table 1.2 Examples of vocal tics ||
Simple vocal tics	Complex vocal tics
Throat clearing	Phrases:
Coughing	'Oh boy'
Spitting	'Shut up'
Sniffing	'You know'
Snorting	'All right'
Screeching	Animal noises
Barking	Muttering under one's breath
Grunting	Complex breathing patterns
Clacking	Stuttering
Whistling	Speech atypicalities including variation in:
Sucking sounds	Accents
Syllable sounds such as 'uh, uh' or 'eee' and 'bu'	Loudness
	Rapidity
	Tones
	Rhythms
	Coprolalia
	Palilalia
	Echolalia

Other complex vocal tics include differences in articulation of speech, such as variation in the rhythm, tone and rate, as well as coprolalia (repetitive use of obscene or socially unacceptable words or phrases). (See Table 1.3.)

Table 1.3 Types of vocal tics
Simple vocal tics – meaningless sounds and noises
Complex vocal tics – utterance of words, phrases or statements
Coprolalia – utterance of obscene, aggressive or socially inappropriate words or phrases
Palilalia – repeating of one's own words or phrases
Echolalia – repeating of words or parts of words of others
Speech atypicalities – unusual rhythms, tone, accents, loudness and very rapid speech

Transient tic disorders

These tics occur mainly during childhood, only last a few weeks or months and are usually confined to the face and neck but may vary. Usually they comprise of motor tics but sometimes vocal tics can exist on their own. The age of onset is usually three to ten years, with more boys being affected than girls. While transient tics by definition do not persist for more than a year, it is not uncommon for a child to have a series of transient tics over the course of several years. In some cases, the tics go unnoticed.

Chronic motor or vocal tics

These tics occur for more than a year and, unlike transient tics, tend not to vary in site. Chronic tics include blinking or neck movements.

Community surveys indicate that between 1 and 12 per cent of children manifest some form of transient or chronic motor tic.

Tourette Syndrome (combined multiple motor and vocal tics)

Tourette Syndrome is described as combined motor and vocal tics which have been present for at least one year. Table 1.4 shows the diagnostic criteria for Tourette Syndrome.

Table 1.4 Diagnostic criteria for Tourette Syndrome

A. Multiple motor tics and one or more vocal tics have been present at some time during the disorder, but not necessarily concurrently.

B. The frequency of tics must be many times a day, nearly every day, for more than one year, with no period of remission during that year lasting longer than two months.

C. The anatomical location, number, frequency, type, complexity or severity of tics must change over time.

D. Onset is before the age of 21 years.

E. The tics must not be explicable by other medical conditions.

Adapted from World Health Organization (1992) and The Tourette Syndrome Classification Study Group (1993)

The onset of tics is usually mild and infrequent and occurs between ages two and twenty-one, with a mean age of onset around age seven (Robertson 1994).

A typical clinical history will be of tic symptoms that usually fluctuate in severity and frequency during the day as well as between days. This fluctuation is often referred to as 'waxing and waning'.

People with Tourette Syndrome often describe a premonitory feeling or sensation prior to the tics, which is separate to the actual tic itself. The sensation is temporarily relieved after the tic has been discharged. Examples of these sensations include a burning feeling in the eye prior to an eye blink, itching before a movement of the shoulders, and tension in the neck that is relieved by stretching the neck.

Tics often increase in severity up to and during puberty. They often reach a relatively stable plateau during early adulthood.

The person with Tourette Syndrome is likely to have a number of different motor and vocal tics but head and neck tics are by far the commonest. Coprolalia rarely occurs in young children and only occurs in 10 to 30 per cent of adult clinic populations and thus this does not need to be present for a diagnosis to be made (Robertson 1994).

Most people can suppress tics for a short period of time only. Many people with Tourette Syndrome find that when they are concentrating on a particular task (such as playing a computer game) their tics seem to decrease in intensity.

The tics may increase during times when children have relaxed after a stressful period, such as when they are returning home from school.

In the past it was thought that tics disappear during sleep but recent studies have shown that tics persist during all stages of sleep (Rothenberger *et al.* 2001).

Epidemiology

Tics are common in childhood and are regarded as part of normal development. It has been estimated that as many as 10 per cent of children have had a tic at some point before the age of ten years. However, these tics are typically transient and fade away within a few months.

Tourette Syndrome occurs in all cultures and racial groups. It is reported to be three to four times more common in males (Robertson 2000).

Studies of school-aged children estimate the prevalence of Tourette Syndrome to be between 0.15 and 1.85 per cent (Hornsey et al. 2001; Kadesjo and Gillberg 2000). However, estimates vary markedly, with some estimates as high as 4.2 per cent of children when all types of tic disorders are included. A wide variation in variables, including different methods of identifying cases and different clinical criteria, account for the different prevalence values.

The prevalence of Tourette Syndrome in children attending special schools is higher than that in children at mainstream schools (Eapen et al. 1997). For example, 8 per cent of children with autistic spectrum disorders in a special school have been shown to have Tourette Syndrome (Baron-Cohen et al. 1999).

Aetiology

Although the precise aetiology is not known, several studies support the fact that Tourette Syndrome is an inherited developmental disorder that involves an imbalance in the transportation of a chemical neurotransmitter, known as dopamine, in the brain (Leckman et al. 2001).

GENETICS

There is no doubt that the development of Tourette Syndrome is genetically determined. What is in doubt is which genes are involved and what the precise mode of inheritance is.

The concordance rate for Tourette Syndrome (in other words if one twin has the syndrome the other will too) is greater than 50 per cent for monozygotic (identical) twins whereas it is 10 per cent for dizygotic (non-identical) twins. If twins with chronic motor tic disorder are included, these figures increase to between 77 and 90 per cent for monozygotic twins and 30 per cent for dizygotic twins (Hyde *et al.* 1992).

Several studies have looked at specific genes but so far no single gene has been consistently identified with Tourette Syndrome. There is also likely to be a genetic component linking Tourette Syndrome, chronic motor tics and Obsessive Compulsive Disorder (OCD) (Eapen, Pauls and Robertson 1993).

NEUROCHEMISTRY

Medication such as neuroleptics (see Chapter 2) (which decrease the availability of dopamine to the brain) decreases the frequency and intensity of tics. This suggests that an alteration in the dopamine levels in the brain has a part to play in the development of tics and Tourette Syndrome. Increased tics have been reported following exposure to agents that increase central dopaminergic activity, such as L-dopa and central nervous system stimulants, including cocaine.

Some neuroimaging studies have demonstrated abnormalities in the way dopamine is transported in the brain. The studies have reported an increased density of the pre-synaptic dopamine transporter and the post-synaptic D2 dopamine receptor and have suggested that there is abnormal regulation of dopamine release and uptake in Tourette Syndrome (Wolf *et al.* 1996).

Post-mortem studies have shown low levels of the neurotransmitter serotonin in the brain stem and low levels of glutamate in a part of the brain known as the globus pallidus (Singer 2000). Serotonin has been shown to be important in the development of the condition OCD but there is no evidence that medication that improves OCD, i.e. increases the availability of serotonin in the brain, has an effect on tics.

NEUROIMAGING

Since Tourette Syndrome is a complex condition involving difficulties with motor control, impulse control, premonitory urges and vocal tics which may involve emotionally charged words, it is likely that several regions and pathways of the brain are involved. Table 1.5 shows the main pathways and regions of the brain that are reported to be involved in Tourette Syndrome. For details of specific studies see Peterson and Thomas (2000).

Table 1.5 Regions and pathways of the brain that are involved in Tourette Syndrome

Subcortical nuclei – includes basal ganglia (caudate, putamen and globus pallidus) and thalamus

Orbitofrontal pathways

Sensorimotor pathways

Temporolimbic pathways

Cingulate cortex

Brainstem motor nuclei

There are many limitations when looking at the neuroimaging studies of Tourette Syndrome. Most of the studies have been carried out on adults in a clinic population. This means that studies include a bias of patients who are more likely to have severe symptoms. Regarding neuroimaging studies in children, the brain is still developing right up until late adolescence so it is difficult to make precise interpretations. Most studies tend to be of small numbers of people so it is difficult to make useful statistical generalizations.

Structural neuroimaging studies (studies looking directly at the structures in the brain such as Computerized Tomography (CT) and Magnetic Resonance Imaging (MRI)), which compare patients with Tourette Syndrome with age-matched controls, show that the caudate nucleus size is reduced in both adults and children with Tourette Syndrome. The lenticular nucleus volumes are found to be reduced in adults with Tourette Syndrome (Gerard and Peterson 2003).

A study looking at cortical regions found that children with Tourette Syndrome had an enlarged pre-frontal cortical volume compared to healthy controls (Peterson *et al.* 2001). Age correlated inversely with pre-frontal volume so that by adulthood, patients had smaller pre-frontal volumes than did controls. Peterson *et al.* (2001) suggest that the pre-frontal area is strongly activated when suppressing tic symptoms and the larger pre-frontal volumes in children probably represents an activity-dependent plastic change of pre-frontal tissues that help individuals with tics to suppress and compensate for their symptoms.

Most functional neuroimaging studies (studies looking at the working components of the brain, measuring blood flow or metabolism) have shown that metabolism and regional cerebral blood flow are generally reduced in parts of the basal ganglia in adults with Tourette Syndrome (Hall, Costa and Shields 1990; Moriarty *et al.* 1995).

PERINATAL FACTORS

Much research is still needed in this area; however, there have been a few studies which have found interesting results in relation to perinatal factors associated with Tourette Syndrome. Two studies have shown that Tourette Syndrome is associated with low birth weight (Hyde *et al.* 1992; Leckman *et al.* 1987). Other factors include maternal stress during pregnancy and severe vomiting or nausea in the first trimester (Leckman *et al.* 1990). These studies indicate the above factors are only associated with Tourette Syndrome and are not a direct cause of the condition.

Paediatric Autoimmune Neuropsychiatric Disorders Associated with Streptococcal Infection (PANDAS)

There have been recent studies over the last few years linking the sudden onset of obsessive compulsive symptoms and/or tics with Group A Haemolytic Streptococcal Infection (GABHS). The term for this condition is Paediatric Autoimmune Neuropsychiatric Disorders Associated with Streptococcal Infection (PANDAS). The diagnostic criteria include (Swedo *et al.* 1998):

1. the presence of OCD and/or tics

2. pre-pubertal age at onset

3. sudden onset and remission of symptoms

4. a temporal relationship between symptoms and GABHS

5. the presence of neurological abnormalities including hyperactivity and choreiform movements.

The evidence that a specific condition is related to streptococcal infection is based on a number of clinical and neuroimmunological findings. Volumetric MRI analysis of children with PANDAS showed that basal ganglia structures were significantly larger than in a healthy control group (Giedd *et al.* 2000). It has been proposed that an immune-mediated mechanism similar to the mechanism in another medical condition, Sydenham's chorea, occurs in which antibodies produced against GABHS cross-react with neuronal tissue in the basal ganglia (Singer *et al.* 1999). However, despite these studies there have been no prospective epidemiological studies linking tic disorders/OCD directly with streptococcal infections.

There are also numerous case reports of other conditions arising as a result of a post-streptococcal autoimmune disorder (Dale *et al.* 2002; DiFazio, Morales and Davis 1998; Sokol 2000), so the association with streptococcal infections does not appear to be specific.

The difficulty with confirming that this condition exists is the problem of identifying a clear association between streptococcal infections and tics since both tics and streptococcal infections are common in paediatric populations.

For the time being, it may be worth simply documenting whether the onset or worsening of tics coincides with a throat infection or related illness. Further research is needed in this interesting but still speculative area.

Prognosis

Tics usually start in early childhood and then gradually increase in intensity and severity as the child approaches adolescence, usually peaking in severity by mid-adolescence. During this period there may be frequent periods of fluctuations. By early adulthood tics then tend to decrease in frequency and forcefulness. The prognosis is better than previously thought, with around 90 per cent of people with Tourette Syndrome experiencing substantial remission; more than 40 per cent of children will be predominantly tic-free by age 18 (Burd *et al.* 2001; Leckman *et al.* 1998).

Stress has a part to play in exacerbating the tics and there are numerous case reports of tics temporarily worsening in later life after some sort of traumatic event such as bereavement or personal illness. However, the precise relationship between individual stress factors and tics has not really been established.

Clinical assessment

The assessment of a child with tics involves compiling a detailed clinical history followed by a neurological examination. It is useful to note down whether any tics actually occur in the clinic, although many children do suppress tics when they meet professionals for the first time. The description of clinical symptoms should determine whether a child has transient tics, chronic tics or Tourette Syndrome. The ability of patients to suppress their tics helps to differentiate tics from other movement disorders such as chorea, dystonia, athetosis and myoclonus (Demirkiran and Jankovic 1995). (For descriptions of movement disorders other than tics see Table 1.6.)

The site, severity and frequency of tics as well as precipitating and relieving factors should be recorded.

Associated symptoms such as those of Attention Deficit Hyperactivity Disorder (ADHD) and Obsessive Compulsive Disorder (OCD) should also be noted (see Chapter 3). Other associated symptoms include self-harming, poor sleep and secondary depression. In many cases, the tics are not the main

Table 1.6 Other movement disorders

Dystonia – a sustained muscle contraction leading to repetitive movements or abnormal postures

Chorea – involuntary, abrupt, irregular and random movements

Athetosis – slow, sinuous, writhing movements performed involuntarily and especially severe in the hands

Tremor – rhythmic oscillation of a body part produced by alternating or synchronous contraction of antagonistic muscles

Myoclonus – brief, sudden, shock-like movements caused by active muscle contraction

problem but the related behaviour, such as impulsivity, aggression and rage, cause most of the difficulties.

The clinician should obtain a detailed account of precipitating events and maintaining factors for inappropriate behaviour and rage. Is there anything that helps and how is it handled? Ask the child what he thinks of the tics and how he deals with them. What makes the child relax? How do other members of the family react to the tics?

A family history of tics or OCD should be recorded.

A medication history is important especially since some children with ADHD may have been prescribed stimulant medication, which in turn can precipitate or exacerbate tics in children who are predisposed to tic disorders. School-related issues worth asking about include whether there is any bullying and teasing taking place. The clinician should enquire about the child's academic performance, including concentration and motivation. Does the child have problems with gross and fine motor coordination? This may show itself with problems with handwriting (fine motor skills) and difficulties in the gym and the sports field (gross motor coordination).

An assessment is complete with a mental state examination (including assessing the child's mood and self-esteem) and a neurological examination of the child.

Key questions that need to be addressed for the purposes of managing the tics include:

1. Do the tics cause impairment of daily functioning at home or at school?

2. Are the tics painful?

3. Is there bullying and teasing?

4. How does the child cope with the tics?

5. What is the child's self-esteem like?

The use of rating scales

A number of assessment tools exist which help clarify the diagnosis, but they are also useful to monitor progress and for research purposes. These include:

- the Motor Tic, Obsessions and Compulsions, Vocal Tic Evaluation Survey (MOVES) (Gaffney, Sieg and Hellings 1994)

- the National Hospital Interview Schedule (NHIS) (Robertson and Eapen 1996)

- the Yale Global Tic Severity Scale (YGTSS) (Leckman *et al.* 1989).

Other causes of tics

As well as OCD and ADHD, there are a number of other neuropsychiatric disorders in which tics appear, including schizophrenia and autistic spectrum disorders.

Tics can also occur secondary to a number of factors (Kumar and Lang 1997). Most of the conditions and factors are uncommon and there are usually other features of systemic illness present which should easily differentiate them from Tourette Syndrome.

- Infections giving rise to tics are rare but include Sydenham's Chorea (streptococcal infection), Creutzfeldt- Jakob Disease, neurosyphilis and various forms of encephalitis.

- Toxic states, such as carbon monoxide poisoning, can give rise to tics, as does hypoglycaemia.

- Drugs that cause tics include antipsychotics, antidepressants, lithium, stimulants (methylphenidate) and antiepileptics.

- Inherited disorders that may show tics include Huntington's Disease, tuberous sclerosis, Wilson's Disease and chromosomal disorders such as Down Syndrome, Klinefelter's Syndrome and Fragile X.

- Acquired causes include head injury and cerebrovascular accidents.

CHAPTER TWO

Psychological and Medical Management

Introduction

The majority of tic disorders, including Tourette Syndrome, need little intervention. The reassurance of the child and family and their education on the condition are often all that is required. Most parents say that educating the respective relatives, teachers and public is also crucial in most cases. However, if the tics are painful, causing psychological distress or simply making the child's life miserable, then more direct intervention is needed.

The goal is not to eliminate all tics completely, but to relieve tic-related discomfort or embarrassment and for the child to achieve a degree of control of tics that allows him to function as normally as possible.

The use of medication has been the main form of treatment in the UK. Sometimes psychological tips and techniques may be helpful to reduce the intensity and frequency of tics but the research on this is sparse and under reported. Management of associated features such as symptoms of Attention Deficit Hyperactivity Disorder (ADHD) and Obsessive Compulsive Disorder (OCD) should also be considered. Parents and clinicians should also be aware of other ways in which a child can be helped, such as anger management, help with education and improving self-esteem. These topics are covered in subsequent chapters.

Reassurance and psychoeducation

Once a diagnosis of Tourette Syndrome is made, it is important that the family members are aware of the natural history of the condition and the related clinical symptoms. The tics will vary in location, frequency and intensity and the natural course is that they will wax and wane. Family members and teachers need to be reminded that tics should not be regarded as wilful behaviours. A useful analogy is that of eye blinking: 'We all have the ability to temporarily suppress eye blinking but eventually and inevitably we do give in to the need to blink' (Peterson and Cohen 1998, p.65).

It is important that families gain a brief understanding of the biological basis of Tourette Syndrome as, apart from anything else, this helps to reinforce the fact that the child does not have full control of the tics. Families often find it useful to hear that Tourette Syndrome is by no means a rare condition and it is likely that Tourette Syndrome is at one end of a spectrum of tic disorders which are more prevalent in the community.

It is important for families to learn that prognosis does not necessarily depend on severity of the tics but on other factors, such as degree of understanding of the condition at home and school, the child's self-esteem and the child's general coping abilities and outlook on life.

In mild cases, a diagnosis and reassurance is all that is required since the child and family may be coping reasonably well without the need for further intervention or treatment. If, however, treatment is warranted, then there is a range of behavioural and medical treatments available.

Psychological intervention

There have been relatively few studies showing that psychological therapies can be effective at reducing tics (Robertson 2000). Many of the published reports have limitations in their methodologies and they contain only small numbers of patients. There are also very few trained clinicians who could administer the psychological therapies, even if their efficacies were firmly established. Thus, although a lot of parents would prefer non-medical interventions for their children, it is unfortunate that the usefulness of psychological therapies is not well established. Nevertheless, knowledge of some simple psychological techniques may be helpful to complement the use of medication and sometimes may be all that is needed for children with mild tics.

Stress can precipitate and worsen tics and thus reduction of stress will be beneficial. A psychological assessment should focus on the precipitating stressful factors, including looking closely at any environmental circumstances which make tics worse. For instance, are tics worse in a particular place, such as school hall, home or shops? Is there a temporal pattern to the tics? Do they occur in the morning, at lunchtime, or only on school days? The majority of tics that appear in Tourette Syndrome have no particular pattern, although stress can make tics more prominent. Identifying stressful situations will then enable one to develop strategies that focus on reducing stress in that particular situation.

John's tics seemed to increase first thing in the morning on school days but improved as the day went on. The increase had been put down to John's anxieties about his academic abilities in the classroom. On further questioning, it transpired that it was not the school lessons themselves that caused so much stress in the morning but it was the fact that he had to sit perfectly still in the school assembly in front of the teachers. John's allocated seat in the assembly hall was right in the middle of the hall. He often felt trapped and enclosed and was terrified that he could not control his motor and vocal tics. He was self-conscious and felt that the teachers and fellow pupils were staring at him.

Once this was recognized, the school psychologist suggested that John sit near the door at the edge of the assembly hall. Thus, if he felt the urge to release a tic, he could go out of the hall without creating any fuss. Subsequently, John's tics decreased in the morning as he became more relaxed about the school assembly.

As with all therapies, prior to any intervention, it is advisable to establish an initial baseline of tic frequency and intensity in order to measure progress.

Relaxation

As mentioned above, anything that helps a child relax may be beneficial to him. This can be something simple such as a massage, having a bath or listening to music. Relaxation combined with concentration on enjoyable tasks may help reduce tic symptom severity. Examples of this include playing computer games or watching television.

Exercise

Some children may benefit from doing exercise and releasing pent-up energy. This can be done during time-out breaks at school or letting the child run out in the local playing fields or parks. Using a punch bag is a good way of releasing energy and can also be useful for anger management.

Guided imagery

Many parents are aware that when their child is absorbed in playing a computer game, the tics seem to disappear for a short period of time. The reason for this is still unknown but it may be due to focused visual attention on the computer screen. Guided imagery uses principles that are similar to this process. This technique involves sustained, relaxed attention to pleasant imaginary scenes without the mention of an explicit suggestion for tic reduction. For example, get the child to picture a quiet beach and imagine the sound of the gentle waves lapping the shore. This will set the scene for further relaxation. Use of relaxation tapes that involve guided imagery may also be helpful.

Massed practice

Some children find it helpful to 'practise' particular tics before going to school or during the school break. For instance, if a child has a tic that involves rolling his shoulders, he could actively roll his shoulders several times in a quiet part of the school. This then causes a natural period of rest for that particular tic and may help the child be tic-free for a short period of time. This might be useful prior to stressful situations such as exams or performing on stage.

Habit reversal

This technique was developed by Azrin and Nunn (1973) and consists of five components. The first is monitoring and assessing the tics. The second involves focused attention training so the child is aware of all the details of the particular tic. The third component is the selection of an alternative response to the tic, for example contracting the neck instead of head nodding. The fourth and fifth components involve relaxation and motivational training. The main emphasis is on the third component, the selection of an alternative, yet more socially acceptable, response. This may include replacing the tic with another tension movement such as clenching the fist to replace a tic that involves pulling the hair.

The original intention of habit reversal was to replace the particular tic with a competing antagonistic action. For example, paced, soft blinking could replace eye-blinking tics. However, this inhibition may prevent tic onset but may also lead to tension and general discomfort.

If one is aware of a preceding sensory stimulus then concentrating on relaxing a particular muscle when the sensory stimulus arises may be a better method of reducing the tic (Evers and van de Wetering 1994; O'Connor and Gareau 1994).

Medication

The first thing to get clear is that there is no magic cure for tics. Medication can help reduce the intensity of the tics; however, it is unlikely that medication will make tics stop altogether.

Parents should be aware from the outset that the aim of using medication is to allow the child to at least function with minimum impairment at home and at school. Parents and clinicians should be aware that some children with a range of symptoms might not respond at all to medication.

The lowest dosage of medication should always be used initially. The dose should then be adjusted as necessary to achieve a therapeutic effect. This of course needs to be monitored in case of possible side-effects. Parents and children should again be reminded of the nature of tics, i.e. that the condition will wax and wane despite the introduction of medication. One needs to be aware of this phenomenon as the decrease in symptoms may be due to the natural fading of tics and not simply because the child has just started medication.

The main group of medicines used in children are the neuroleptics (haloperidol, pimozide, sulpiride and risperidone) and clonidine. There is no universal agreement on first-line drug of choice. The drugs are usually prescribed according to the clinician's experience balanced with side-effect profile. If one drug is not having an effect after a reasonable trial, then changing to another is suggested.

The following contains brief details on these medicines as well as side-effect profiles. Clinicians should check with up-to-date product information and national guidelines when prescribing medicines.

Neuroleptics

The neuroleptic classification of drugs is most often used in adults with psychotic illnesses such as schizophrenia and mania. They were also the first drugs that were shown to reduce tics in Tourette Syndrome. They act primarily by interfering with dopaminergic transmission in the brain by blocking dopamine receptors. They are therefore called dopamine antagonists.

SIDE-EFFECTS OF NEUROLEPTICS

Side-effects include movement disorders such as acute dystonia (sustained muscle contraction) and akathisia (motor restlessness – which tends to occur after initial doses). Long-term use can lead to tardive dyskinesia (rhythmic, involuntary movements of tongue, face and jaw); however, there have been some cases after only short-term treatment on low doses. Tardive dyskinesia is a major concern since it may be irreversible on withdrawing medication, so close monitoring is needed. Some manufacturers suggest withdrawal of the drug is recommended on early signs of tardive dyskinesia, which include fine movements of the tongue.

Dystonias, akathisia, tardive dyskinesia and parkinsonian symptoms (tremor, shuffling gait) are collectively known as 'extrapyramidal symptoms'. The clinician should enquire about side-effects such as movement difficulties when reviewing medication.

Other side-effects include hypotension (abnormally low blood pressure), drowsiness, dry mouth, constipation and blurred vision. Occasionally social and school phobia can develop which disappears when medication is discontinued. Amenorrhoea (cessation of menstruation), galactorrhoea (excessive lactation) and gynaecomastia (enlargement of breasts) are also recognized side-effects of the neuroleptics.

The neuroleptic malignant syndrome is a rare but potentially fatal adverse effect of neuroleptic medication. It is an idiosyncratic reaction to neuroleptics characterized by muscular rigidity, fever, labile blood pressure, sweating, urinary incontinence and fluctuating levels of consciousness. Blood tests reveal that there is a raised level of creatine phosphokinase (an enzyme contained in the muscles that is released into the bloodstream when a particular muscle is damaged). Discontinuation of the neuroleptic in such a case is essential. Cooling and prescription of drugs such as bromocriptine and amantadine are helpful in reducing symptoms (British National Formulary 2003).

HALOPERIDOL

Trade names: Dozic, Haldol, Halperon, Serenace

This is a butyrophenone derivative and works by blocking dopamine D2 receptors in the brain. It has been widely prescribed for tics in most countries. It is said to decrease tic severity in 70 per cent of patients. Despite its good efficacy, care needs to be taken due to problems with unacceptable side-effects. Long-term use requires careful monitoring.

Side-effects
As above.

PIMOZIDE

Trade name: Orap

Pimozide is a diphenylbutylpiperidine derivative, and is prescribed more frequently in the USA than the UK. It has a preference for blocking dopamine D1 receptors in the brain. It has been shown to be slightly more effective than haloperidol and also produces similar but fewer side-effects. However, due to concerns with cardiac side-effects, pimozide is not recommended for children.

Side-effects

Pimozide produces similar side-effects to haloperidol. In addition it is associated with a variety of electrocardiograph (ECG) changes that require monitoring. There is thus a risk of potentially fatal cardiac arrhythmias. It is recommended that anyone starting on pimozide should have an initial ECG and regular check-ups.

SULPIRIDE

Trade names: Dolmatil, Sulparex, Sulpitil

Sulpiride is a substituted benzamide derivative. It is a selective D2 antagonist. It has been mainly studied in adults but, because it has fewer side-effects than haloperidol, it is now prescribed for children.

Side-effects

Similar to haloperidol but less extrapyramidal symptoms.

RISPERIDONE

Trade name: Risperdal

Risperidone is a benzisoxazole derivative. It is considered an 'atypical' neuroleptic as opposed to haloperidol and pimozide (dopamine D2 blockers), which are the 'typical' neuroleptics. It binds strongly to serotonin receptors and thus is described as having a high affinity. It prevents the release of serotonin and is thus termed an antagonist of the serotonin 5-HT2 receptors. It does not block as much release of dopamine and is thus a weaker antagonist than haloperidol. Its mechanism of action in treating tic disorders is unknown, although it may derive some of its efficacy through blocking of serotoninergic projections to the ventral striatum, a brain region implicated in the pathophysiology of Tourette Syndrome. The blocking of D2 receptors, although weak, is also said to account for its efficacy. It is also helpful for reducing aggression.

Side-effects

It has similar side-effects to haloperidol but less extra-pyramidal side-effects. Significant weight gain even on relatively low dosage is a major concern for children and adolescents.

Other medicines

CLONIDINE

Trade names: Catapres, Dixarit

Clonidine is an alpha-2-adrenergic pre-synaptic agonist. It is mainly used for migraine and hypertension (abnormally high blood pressure). Over the last few years it has been widely prescribed in children due to the less harmful side-effects than the neuroleptics. It is particularly beneficial for children with associated ADHD symptoms. It is recommended that blood pressure is checked when starting the medication with subsequent monitoring at regular intervals or when there is a change to the dose.

Side-effects

Side-effects include drowsiness, depression, low blood pressure, nocturnal unrest and Raynaud's phenomenon (a condition in which blood flow to the peripheral parts of the body, namely fingers and toes, is restricted resulting in cold and blue extremities).

Because blood pressure may be lowered whilst taking clonidine, sudden withdrawal of the drug can lead to a rapid rise in blood pressure. It is therefore advised that discontinuation of the drug should be done gradually.

LESS COMMONLY USED MEDICINES

These include guanfacine, clonazepam and nicotine.

Medication for tics and ADHD

As mentioned above, clonidine is a useful drug if there are associated ADHD symptoms. This helps reduce hyperactivity but has little effect on poor concentration.

Stimulant medication, such as methylphenidate and dexamphetamine, when used for children with ADHD, may precipitate or worsen tics in some patients. However, this observation alone may not necessarily be a contraindication for its use in Tourette Syndrome and associated ADHD. Children may benefit enormously if the ADHD symptoms can be reduced. Still, a full explanation should be given to the family and child with medication being stopped if tics worsen. See Chapter 3 for further details.

Medication for tics and OCD

Use of a selective serotonin re-uptake inhibitor, such as fluoxetine or sertraline, may be used to target specific OCD symptoms in patients with Tourette Syndrome and associated OCD. Thus patients with Tourette Syndrome and OCD should have access to pharmacological interventions that are used to treat OCD. See Chapter 3 for further details.

CHAPTER THREE

Associated Conditions

Introduction

Children with Tourette Syndrome sometimes have associated symptoms that include other semi-involuntary behaviours. This includes symptoms of obsessions and compulsions as well as impulsivity and hyperactivity. In many cases, these symptoms are so prominent that a second or associated diagnosis is usually made. The main two conditions associated with Tourette Syndrome are Obsessive Compulsive Disorder and Attention Deficit Hyperactivity Disorder.

Obsessive Compulsive Disorder

Obsessive Compulsive Disorder (OCD) is a condition characterized by unwanted thoughts or images (obsessions) and unwanted repetitive acts and rituals (compulsions). Many people have OCD symptoms and are reluctant to seek help or share their concerns for fear of being ridiculed or stigmatized.

It used to be thought that OCD was a condition that affected adults only but studies in the last 15 years have shown that the condition is prevalent in children, occurring in 1 in 100 children (Heyman *et al.* 2001). It is still debatable as to whether OCD in childhood is exactly the same condition as that in adulthood. The similarities are that both age groups share relatively the same clinical phenotype and both respond to the same pharmacological intervention. However, recent studies (e.g. Geller *et al.* 1998) show that childhood OCD is associated with peaks in age onset indicating a bimodal incidence of the disorder (the peak ages of onset are 10 and 21 years). In the early-onset age group there is a male preponderance and a distinct pattern of comorbidity with tic disorders and Attention Deficit Hyperactivity Disorder. This is in keeping with other neurodevelopmental disorders.

Clinical features

Common obsessions include thoughts on contamination, hoarding, aggressive images or preoccupation with one's body (see Table 3.1). The thoughts are usually recognized as irrational and arising from one's own mind (which distinguishes this from delusions, although younger children may not be able to conceptualize this well).

Compulsions include excessive washing, checking, counting and repeating things (see Table 3.1). The OCD symptoms fall into four main groups:

- checking and ruminations
- symmetry and ordering
- fear of contamination
- hoarding.

In order to meet criteria for a clinical diagnosis, there needs to be some degree of impairment in terms of time consumed with OCD symptoms, and distress or interference in daily functioning (American Psychiatric Association 1994).

Table 3.1 Common obsessions and compulsions	
Obsessions	*Compulsions*
Contamination	Washing
Aggression	Checking
Sexual	Repeating
Hoarding	Needing reassurance
Magical thoughts	Counting
Somatic	Ordering
Religious	Arranging
	Hoarding

It should be remembered that young children go through a developmental phase of behavioural rituals between the ages of two and six years. Childhood rituals differ from OCD since they are not associated with obsessional thoughts, they are easily circumvented by distraction, and anger rather than anxiety is usually their response when they are prevented from doing them.

OCD and Tourette Syndrome

There have been a number of reports looking at the type of obsessions and compulsions seen in children and adults with Tourette Syndrome. Leckman *et al.* (1994) showed that patients with tic-related OCD were more likely to be male and have an earlier age of onset of their OCD symptoms. Patients with tic-related OCD reported increased rates of obsessions related to aggressive and sexual thoughts. Several studies have shown that patients with OCD without tics tend to have more obsessions around contamination and cleaning than those who had OCD with tics (George *et al.* 1993; Holzer *et al.* 1994;

Leckman *et al.* 1994/1995). The compulsions in tic-related OCD tend to be related to touching, hoarding and counting rituals.

Intervention

A measure of the severity of OCD can be obtained by using rating scales and questionnaires such as the Yale Brown Obsessive Compulsive Scale for Children (Scahill *et al.* 1997) or the child version of the Leyton Obsessive Inventory (Berg, Rapoport and Flament 1986).

PSYCHOEDUCATION

This is an important part of the treatment offered. The more one knows about OCD, the more one feels in control; hence a brief explanation of the biological basis for OCD is valuable. This helps to stop the child being labelled as 'naughty' by the parents. In some cases the child and family are reassured within the first session with a full explanation of OCD and require no further intervention.

INDIVIDUAL WORK WITH CHILDREN AND ADOLESCENTS

A good example of individual work with a child is described in protocols (developed by March and Mulle) in the book *OCD in Children and Adolescents: A Cognitive-Behavioural Treatment Manual* (March and Mulle 1998). The techniques for individual work include:

- externalization of OCD

- development of cognitive tactics and coping strategies (a cognitive 'toolkit') to assist with exposure-response prevention (whereby the patient is made to face his anxiety-provoking stiuation without his usual ritualized responses), e.g. positive self-talk (encouraging oneself and looking at things logically)

- increasing self-efficacy

- generating a hierarchy of obsessions and compulsions to tackle (with the child)

- use of exposure-response prevention on targets chosen by the child (usually *in vivo*) and usually with some support from parents.

FAMILY INTERVENTIONS

The family is encouraged to become part of the 'expert team' that helps the child fight OCD and thus can prove to be a useful source of support away from the clinics.

Family members often get caught up in the rituals and routines surrounding OCD and may contribute to the maintenance of symptoms (Waters, Barrett and March 2001). Family-focused interventions on psychosocial factors are also likely to be more effective and durable than interventions that target the child. It has also been shown that high levels of hostility and criticism have been associated with poor treatment outcome and relapse in adults (Chambless and Steketee 1999). Another reason for involving the family is that the rates of OCD among members of the family of someone with OCD are higher than the general population and thus helpful interventions for the targeted individual may have secondary benefits to other potentially vulnerable members.

Family interventions include exploring the effect of OCD on the family, improving coping strategies, improving communication skills, psychoeducation, reducing parental involvement in the symptoms, and increasing positive family interactions. A study by Barrett, Healey-Famel and March (2004) showed that involving the family in cognitive behavioural therapy could be effective. This can be carried out with the individual child and family or in a group therapy format.

MEDICATION

At the time of writing, selective serotonin re-uptake inhibitors (SSRI) such as sertraline and fluoxetine are the drugs often used as first choice. Side-effects include nausea, headache, gastrointestinal complaints, insomnia and agitation. Other drugs include clomipramine, which is a tricyclic antidepressant that is also a serotonin re-uptake inhibitor. The side-effects of this include a dry mouth, dizziness, tremor, constipation and gastrointestinal discomfort. It is important that the family are informed of potential side-effects that may occur so that the family and child do not lose trust in medication should these occur.

If the child does not respond to one particular SSRI after 10 to 12 weeks, switching to another SSRI would be appropriate (American Academy of Child and Adolescent Psychiatry 1998). A number of children will show no improvement to cognitive behavioural treatment and medication. If a trial of two different SSRIs and cognitive behavioural therapy has been tried for a reasonable length of time with no response, consideration should be given to augmenting this with a low dose of neuroleptic (see Chapter 2).

Children are usually maintained on medication for 12 to 18 months.

LIAISON WITH SCHOOLS AND OTHER SERVICES

OCD can often have an impact on the child's functioning in the classroom and with homework. For instance, children with checking rituals will often re-read a line in a textbook several times until it is 'just right' or a child may need to perform a counting ritual in the classroom before he can sit down. If the child's education is affected, it may be helpful for the clinician, with the child's and parents' permission, to talk to the child's teacher and give a brief explanation of the difficulties.

CHILDREN

Support groups for children with OCD may be a valuable way of increasing awareness and education on aspects of OCD. It can also provide much needed psychosocial support to the often isolated individual.

A lot of support is needed for the child and family and therefore it is often useful to provide details of voluntary organizations such as OCD Action, a UK national charity, which provides information and support for families suffering from OCD (sée Appendix II).

Attention Deficit Hyperactivity Disorder

Attention Deficit Hyperactivity Disorder (ADHD) is a disorder with core symptoms of inattention, hyperactivity and impulsivity, which are present from an early age. These symptoms are common in children but when extreme, cause marked impairment in the child.

ADHD usually begins early in life with symptoms exhibited before seven years of age. It can affect the individual throughout his lifespan, often persisting into adolescence and adulthood. Impaired peer and family relationships may result and there is an increased risk of social isolation. Adverse outcomes include delinquency, antisocial behaviour and academic underachievement.

The prevalence of ADHD varies depending on the method of ascertainment, the diagnostic criteria used and population sampled. Most studies estimate the prevalence to be somewhere between 5 and 10 per cent in boys and 3 and 4 per cent in girls (Dulcan 1997). The prevalence declines with age.

Clinical features

The main features include problems with inattention such as being easily distracted, losing things and not completing tasks, as well as problems with impulsivity and hyperactivity such as interrupting others, fidgeting and having persistent motor activity (American Psychiatric Association 1994). See Table 3.2.

Features of ADHD vary within and among individual children. The characteristics are usually pervasive across situations, which means the child is likely to have problems both at home and at school.

Children with ADHD are overactive. Overactivity is motor activity displayed by a child that is excessive and inappropriate for a given situation. What counts as excessive motor activity will vary according to the age and developmental stage of the child. In pre-school years, the child is described as always rushing around and climbing on furniture. The staff make frequent comments on how noisy and boisterous the child is. At school, the teachers describe the child as being fidgety, squirming in his chair, being restless and having an inability to remain in his classroom seat. The child is easily distracted by irrelevant stimuli. He also loses things such as school equipment, gym kit and personal possessions.

Table 3.2 Clinical features of ADHD

Careless with detail

Fails to sustain attention

Appears not to listen

Does not finish instructed task

Poor self-organization

Avoids tasks that require sustained mental effort

Loses things

Easily distracted

Seems forgetful

Fidgets all the time

Leaves seat when should be seated

Runs/climbs excessively and inappropriately

Noisy in play

Persistent overactivity unmodified by social context

Blurts out answers before questions completed

Fails to wait turn or in a queue

Interrupts others' conversation or games

Talks excessively

Hyperactive children tend to have difficulty getting off to sleep. When they do go to sleep they often need less sleep than their peers and hence wake up early.

The child's impulsive nature leads him to be reckless and accident prone, and to pay little heed to social rules.

Other features include emotional excitability, increased rate of tantrums, attention-seeking behaviour, inability to learn from punishment and poor social skills (Hill and Cameron 1999).

ADHD and Tourette Syndrome

ADHD occurs in many children with Tourette Syndrome. Studies have shown a wide variation in prevalence ranging from 21 to 90 per cent in clinic samples (Robertson 2000). It is likely that it is the ADHD symptoms that cause the child with Tourette Syndrome to have difficulty coping and therefore clinic samples contain a large cohort of children with both diagnoses.

Treatment

EDUCATION

Once a diagnosis is made, an explanation and information about ADHD should be given to the child and parents. Information sheets and telephone numbers for support groups may be all that is needed (see Appendix II).

PSYCHOSOCIAL INTERACTION

Training parents and teaching them behavioural interventions can often help families cope with the hyperactive child. This involves:

- identifying specific behaviour problems
- using positive reinforcement for appropriate behaviours
- enhancing parental skills during play
- improving effective methods of communicating, such as making eye contact with the child and not using too many commands.

SCHOOL-BASED INTERVENTIONS

Simple interventions include having the child seated close to the teacher and away from distractions such as the window and other similar children. The academic work may need to be broken down in 'chunks' so the child does not get too overwhelmed and is able to manage in comparison to his peers.

BEHAVIOURAL INTERVENTIONS AT HOME

Cognitive and behavioural interventions can be effective for milder cases. However, they need to be applied consistently over a long period of time.

BEHAVIOURAL MANAGEMENT TECHNIQUES

These are focused on parents and encourages them to use basic strategies such as praise and rewards when the child enacts the desired behaviour (i.e. increases his attention to a specific task) in contrast to criticism or arguments. It is important to have realistic expectations of behaviour; for example, if concentration is for two minutes, an increase to three minutes should be praised. Reinforcement of the desired behaviour should be clear and immediate. Research has shown that behavioural techniques often work better when the child is also on medication.

MEDICATION

Stimulants such as methylphenidate and dexamphetamine are the first drugs of choice used in treating ADHD. The National Institute for Clinical Excellence (NICE) in the UK has produced a guideline on the use of methylphenidate for ADHD (NICE 2000). NICE is a statutory government-funded advisory body established within the National Health Service in England and Wales to provide advice and guidance for clinicians and patients on a wide range of health issues. The report emphasizes the need for a detailed assessment of children with ADHD. It also stated that methylphenidate is recommended for use as part of a comprehensive treatment for children with severe ADHD. Studies have clearly shown that use of methylphenidate is effective in children with ADHD (The MTA Cooperative Group 1999).

Main side-effects include poor appetite, loss of sleep and tics.

Clonidine (see Chapter 2) is particularly useful in children with ADHD and comorbid tics or where there are sleep problems. Other forms of medication include tricyclic antidepressants such as imipramine or desipramine (Taylor *et al.* 1998).

Children on medication for ADHD should be regularly reviewed and any side-effects should be monitored. An initial trial period of two weeks with titration of dose is usually sufficient to establish if there has been a response. Conners' parent and teacher questionnaires (Conners 1997) and other rating scales are helpful for establishing any change in behaviour. Once an effective dose has been established, follow-up appointments can be at monthly to six-monthly intervals.

DIET

Some parents comment that certain food additives are associated with an increase in hyperactivity, such as E numbers and flavourings. If parents have noted any particular reaction to particular foods then these foods can be avoided. However, if there is to be a proper trial of dietary manipulation then a paediatric dietician should be involved to ensure that the child has adequate nutrition. At the time of writing, there is no consistent scientific evidence to say that food additives cause hyperactivity.

Prognosis

Without intervention, children with ADHD have been shown to become more oppositional and defiant during their middle childhood and may show antisocial behaviour in adolescence. Many children with ADHD will show antisocial behaviour in adulthood (Simonoff *et al.* 2004).

There is also likely to be progressive educational underachievement and this is also linked with low self-esteem. Up to 65 per cent of children will have features of ADHD extending into adulthood. Specific predictors of poor prognosis include oppositional and aggressive behaviour, low IQ and poor peer relations (Dulcan 1997).

The evidence that an early introduction of medication alters prognosis is limited. However, it is still important that the condition is recognized so that related issues such as educational difficulties and low self-esteem can be addressed.

Depression

A lot of children feel sad and depressed if they are experiencing something upsetting or stressful. Usually these feelings are short lived. If the feeling of sadness continues, and it starts to interfere with daily life, then the child may be suffering from clinical depression. The main features of this are:

- feeling unhappy and miserable

- lacking any sense of enjoyment in usual hobbies or interests

- having difficulty concentrating

- becoming withdrawn

- becoming more self-critical and blaming oneself

- experiencing tiredness and no energy

- starting to become more withdrawn

- feeling hopeless

- having thoughts of self-harm.

Some studies have shown an increased rate of depression in children and adults with Tourette Syndrome (Robertson *et al.* 1997; Wodrich, Benjamin and Lachar 1997).

It is not clear whether the depression is as a result of the tic disorder – i.e. a chronic disabling condition – or due to other associated factors such as being bullied.

It is important to note that the medication that is used to control tics in Tourette Syndrome, such as clonidine, can give rise to depression. The depression tends to improve once medication is reduced or stopped.

Treatment for clinical depression includes counselling, cognitive therapy, individual psychotherapy and anti-depressants.

Anxiety

Anxiety-related conditions such as generalized anxiety disorder, panic attacks and phobias are seen often in children and adults with Tourette Syndrome. The symptoms usually involve excessive worrying and fear about something. Physical symptoms include breathlessness, palpitations, a dry mouth and stomach pains. Several studies have indicated that anxiety symptoms in Tourette Syndrome may be so great as to have an impact on daily life (Comings and Comings 1987; Robertson *et al.* 1997).

Side-effects of neuroleptics such as haloperidol include school phobia. Other side-effects such as akathisia (restlessness) may mimic anxiety.

Rage

Several studies have shown that children with Tourette Syndrome who have been seen at specialist clinics may suffer from recurrent episodes of explosive anger or 'rage' attacks (Budman *et al.* 2000; Wand *et al.* 1993). It is often these attacks that are the most worrying for parents. The research indicates that children with Tourette Syndrome without any associated features of ADHD or OCD are unlikely to have problems with rage episodes.

Many parents and teachers describe seeing some children totally lose control and throw things, shouting, kicking and screaming. It may be a minor event that has precipitated the rage. The episode may last for some time.

It is unclear what causes these rage episodes but it may be the fact that the child has been desperately using his energy to keep his tics under control and it becomes too overwhelming.

Immediate intervention may be necessary if there is a question of safety to the child or others. The best intervention is to allow the child to settle down in a safe place. It is important that the safe place is not a small and confined room that may increase the child's feeling of being restricted.

Oppositional behaviour

Oppositional behaviour involves persistent, defiant behaviour including frequent arguments with adults, often losing one's temper, deliberately annoying others, actively refusing to comply with adults' requests, being easily annoyed by others and being spiteful and vindictive on a regular basis. A collection of these symptoms make up the condition Oppositional Defiant Disorder which is listed in the *Diagnostic and Statistical Manual of Mental Disorders* (American Psychiatric Association 1994). There is some disagreement amongst clinicians as to whether this should be a separate disorder or whether it is a collection of symptoms with different origins. If a child has Tourette Syndrome and some features of oppositional behaviour, one has to seriously think whether giving the child another 'label' such as Oppositional Defiant Disorder is helpful or doing more harm. In any case it is clear that the child and parents need ongoing support.

Sleep difficulties

Many children with Tourette Syndrome have difficulties with sleep. This includes difficulties falling asleep, separation anxiety in the evening and sleep walking. Associated ADHD may also lead to an increase in sleep problems, particularly getting off to sleep.

The sleep difficulties may be so severe that they disrupt family life as well as having a detrimental effect on the child's school performance.

Sleep electro-encephalograph (EEG) findings have shown subtle abnormalities in all stages of sleep (Rothenberger *et al.* 2001). Kostanecka-Endress *et al.* (2003) showed that children with Tourette Syndrome had disturbed sleep patterns with increased arousal.

Medication such as haloperidol and clonidine used to suppress tics may help with sleep difficulties.

Other difficulties

Other associated difficulties may include problems with fine motor coordination leading to handwriting difficulties, problems with social skills and occasionally self-injurious behaviour.

CHAPTER FOUR

Adjusting to the Diagnosis
Parents and Family Members

Introduction

Once a diagnosis of Tourette Syndrome has been made, parents are likely to experience a range of emotions including shock, anger, relief, denial, sadness and guilt. There is no 'correct' way in which to react. Everyone reacts differently in his or her own individual way.

When a diagnosis is made, it is likely that parents may already have some idea that there is something different about their child. They may compare their child to his siblings who behave very differently. Parents may realize that their child stands out amongst his peers and their friends' children. Parents may wonder why they feel so exhausted and tired all the time. They may even resent the fact that other parents seem to have children who are 'not as hard work' and are well behaved. Many parents thus feel a sense of relief when a diagnosis is finally made. They knew something was not quite right about their child and now they have a name for it. Some parents may not be surprised and may already be aware their child has Tourette Syndrome. They may have looked up symptoms on the Internet (NB: it is important to remember that the Internet is not peer reviewed and therefore anyone can write anything about absolutely anything – so care must be taken and do not assume that information is factual just because it is written on the Internet).

Even when parents are sure their child has Tourette Syndrome and are expecting confirmation of the diagnosis, some degree of anxiety takes hold as parents contemplate a future of trying to protect their child.

Some parents see their child very differently from before and go through a period of grief for the loss of the 'perfect child' that they were expecting. Some may find it hard to accept the diagnosis and might seek a second opinion.

It is not unusual for parents to feel angry with professionals, particularly if they have seen several professionals in the past who had put little Liam's problems down to 'parenting issues'. Many parents seen in clinics have wrongly been told by health visitors and doctors that they directly cause their child's behavioural problems.

Some parents may start to fear the worst for their child. They may start to have thoughts that their child is going to be bullied, be unable to hold a job or to have a relationship, and will face a depressing life. If parents do feel any of the above then it is a perfectly normal reaction provided it is short lived. All these emotions take time to work through. The majority of parents will deal with these feelings and adjust and adapt in their own time. Once parents start talking to others in a similar position and start to read more about Tourette Syndrome, they will feel much more confident and reassured.

Parents who are not affected in the slightest way by the diagnosis may be in denial.

Guilt and depression

Many parents of children with Tourette Syndrome feel guilty about their children's condition and behaviour. They may have been told by others that it is their fault that their child behaves in such a 'naughty' way. People automatically assume parents are at fault if they see a child who is acting differently to his peers. There is also no shortage of friends and relatives out there who are only too happy to give advice on how to bring up a child. This is fine if the child has a 'normal' temperament! A lot of children with Tourette Syndrome have 'impulsive' traits and associated features of Attention Deficit Hyperactivity Disorder (ADHD). This is why it takes more effort to control such a child's behaviour and why the advice from relatives is often well meant but ineffective.

Many parents feel guilty since they may have punished their child for tics thinking that the child was deliberately making faces or noises to annoy his parents. Parents may have shouted at the child, taken pocket money away or grounded him. If this is the case, then parents should not feel too guilty. Before a diagnosis was made, how were they to know the tics were part of a disorder over which their child had no control? Unless parents had a degree in the 'study of Tourette Syndrome' then they should not be too hard on themselves.

Parents may also feel guilty because they have read that genes are passed on to children from parents. Occasionally a parent may blame his/her partner for passing on the 'Tourette' gene. Well, to start with, no one has yet found a specific gene that is passed down in Tourette Syndrome. One also forgets that children also inherit from their parents other personality traits such as kindness, patience, thoughtfulness and intelligence.

Some parents may have Tourette Syndrome themselves and may feel convinced that they have passed on the 'Tourette

Syndrome traits', even though there is no evidence for this. These parents know what it is like to live and cope with Tourette Syndrome and so in fact are in a better position than most to give good advice to their child on how to cope and what to look out for. They are also able to empathize with their child, which will help with self-esteem.

If parents consistently feel they are 'bad' parents, cannot think of anything good about themselves and feel guilty most of the time, then they need to see their doctor regarding this. If they also have persistent problems with poor sleep or appetite, and cannot function because of guilt, it may be that they are depressed and need to seek professional help. If they do not seek help and the depression continues, then it may have a negative bearing on their child's behaviour and self-esteem.

The basic message is that all children perform better and are better adjusted when their parents are supportive and strong, and not self-absorbed in their own guilt.

Moving on

Accepting and adapting to a child's diagnosis of Tourette Syndrome takes time. Acceptance does not happen overnight. Talking to people who have been through similar experiences helps. Seeking support from a local Tourette Syndrome group or charity can be valuable. Learn as much as one can about the condition via books and journals. Knowledge is empowerment.

In time, parents will learn that Tourette Syndrome is not as bad as previously imagined. Because of some of the bizarre and colourful symptoms seen in a minority of cases, the media portrayal and public perception of the condition is inaccurate.

The more parents know about the condition, the more they will feel in control. However, parents must learn at their own pace. They should not let it dominate and take over their lives.

With a bit of reading, parents are likely to become experts in Tourette Syndrome. They will probably know more about it than their local doctor. It is not uncommon to hear that parents frequently educate their doctors on the condition. The local doctor is likely to be extremely busy so any up-to-date information on Tourette Syndrome is usually gratefully welcomed. This information may one day help other children to get an earlier diagnosis and receive appropriate management.

Siblings

Once again, different people react in different ways. If a child has Tourette Syndrome, it is likely that his siblings will be affected. This is obviously more so if the child also has features of ADHD.

The sibling may feel annoyed by the vocal tics or irritated by the fact that her brother is always taking her things. She may feel that Mum and Dad give more attention to her brother. She may feel that the sibling with Tourette Syndrome is allowed to get away with things more easily compared to herself.

There is a need to minimize any resentment building up amongst siblings. The sibling should not miss out on any special events because of her brother's Tourette Syndrome. A common example of this is a day trip being cut short and the whole family returning early due to a child's 'difficult' behaviour.

Parents should explain Tourette Syndrome to the sibling. If she is quite young, then tics can be explained as 'hiccups in the brain'. Siblings should also be reminded that the noises their brother makes cannot be controlled.

All fighting incidents should be dealt with fairly. Remember that all siblings fight. Parents of children with Tourette Syndrome need to take extra care and watch out for when their child starts to get just that little bit more excited than usual. Early intervention may save a lot of bother in the long run.

Parents may need to give special time to the sibling since the child with Tourette Syndrome will take up an enormous amount of parents' time. In some cases, the sibling may also feel left out since her brother gets special attention from doctors and teachers.

What can parents do for siblings?

- Remind the sibling of the positive sides to his/her brother.

- Protect the sibling's possessions with special locks.

- Purchase a pair of ear plugs for the sibling.

- When siblings bring friends round to the house, arrange for their brother with Tourette Syndrome to be occupied or distracted.

- Talk to the sibling about her brother's condition.

- Make sure that if a child is responsible for damaging his sibling's possessions and property, then he is also responsible for replacing things – i.e. he has to do chores around the house to earn enough to pay for any damaged items.

- Make sure the sibling has some 'one-to-one' attention at least once a week. This might include going to the shops together or special time at night for story telling.

- Get in touch with a local support group. Some provide meeting places or groups for siblings of children with Tourette Syndrome. Occasionally newsletters feature articles written by siblings of Tourette Syndrome.

- Praise the sibling for staying calm and being patient despite her brother's difficulties.

Relatives

Most family members will be keen to understand about Tourette Syndrome. Parents can provide relatives with information and fact sheets on the condition. There may be some members of the family who refuse to accept the diagnosis through ignorance, denial or simply other unrelated reasons.

Many parents feel let down by some of the attitudes of family members and this sometimes hurts more than anything else. Parents should not expect that everyone will be sympathetic and understanding.

Parents may have to continuously remind certain relatives of the nature of tics. If, after trying to explain a child's condition, parents are still met with scepticism and disapproval, then the parents have to consider whether their child is suffering or experiencing any difficulties when in the company of these relatives.

Many relatives are often at a loss to know what they can do to help. Provide them with enough information about Tourette Syndrome. Explain to them the nature of the tics and the fact that the child has no real control over them. Emphasize that the child should be treated as normal as possible and that they should not make a big issue out of the tics.

Above all, try and keep on good terms with relatives, as it is important for children to feel part of a family system. This is particularly important if the child is isolated from peers in and outside of school. Relatives who understand are also useful people to have as child minders.

Parents and their partners

Looking after a child with Tourette Syndrome can be extremely exhausting. Children need their parents to be strong and supportive. It is therefore vitally important that parents look after themselves.

Some parents, when they learn of their child's diagnosis, feel they cannot enjoy their hobbies and give up previous interests. This may be due to guilt, worry about financial costs or simply the feeling that they have to dedicate every ounce of energy into looking after their child. Unless it is absolutely necessary, parents should not give up on hobbies and interests. Tourette Syndrome should not dominate parents' lives. If it does then it may leave them mentally drained and exhausted.

In order to stay active, fresh and alert:

- Relax – take up yoga, go swimming, go for a walk or take time out to read interesting novels.

- Keep things in perspective – be aware that many children have all sorts of difficulties and that having a child with Tourette Syndrome does not mean that parents have the monopoly on parental stress.

- Talk to others – seek out supportive friends and relatives.

- Talk to other parents in a similar situation – there are many local support groups and charities where parents can contact each other. Seeing others who are in a similar position helps one feel less isolated. Parents may even be able to help other parents by exchanging tips and coping mechanisms.

- If parents have a partner, then it is important to look after each other. Different people will react differently so be sensitive to each other's needs. Recognize that having a child with Tourette Syndrome may bring a great deal of stress to any relationship.

- Treat yourself once in a while. This does not have to be expensive: it can be simply making time for a cup of coffee without being disturbed, buying your favourite magazine, going shopping, or visiting friends.

- Book a child minder or ask a relative to look after your children and go out and enjoy yourself at cinemas, theatres, concerts and restaurants.

A relaxed parent is in a better frame of mind to deal and cope with their child's challenging behaviour.

CHAPTER FIVE

Dealing with Tics and Difficult Behaviour

Introduction

The child has a diagnosis of Tourette Syndrome and he should now get some advice and help from his clinician. Is there any help for parents? The answer is 'yes'. There are ways of coping and adapting to simple tics. Sometimes it is the actual tic that causes distress. At other times it is the associated behavioural difficulties that are the most problematic. A lot of parents also find that dealing with the attitudes of members of the public can be tricky and frustrating. This chapter gives a few simple tips that can help parents survive the day-to-day problems of living with a child with Tourette Syndrome.

Coping with tics

For a child with Tourette Syndrome, tics are part of his everyday make-up and characteristics. He has no control over these tics. There is no point going on at your child about them. He is not doing it on purpose to annoy you. He simply cannot help it. You need to remind yourself that, in the same way, you have no control over your own eye blinking response. If I say to you 'don't blink', you can probably do it for a few seconds, maybe a few minutes, but sooner or later you have to blink. In some instances the child with tics can prevent his tics for a short period of time but sooner or later he has to release the tics regardless. Keep reminding yourself of this analogy.

At home

On the whole, most parents say they can cope with the motor tics as long as they are not painful for the child. If the tic is painful then gentle massage of the muscle with lotion or creams may help. If the pain persists and is unbearable then it is worth visiting the doctor who may prescribe short-term analgesics.

For motor tics that involve the sudden outward movements of limbs it is sensible not to have breakable objects such as vases or ornaments nearby. Be careful also of holding hot cups of tea and coffee near your child. This applies when out in public as well, such as when watching a football match.

Often it is the loud repetitive vocal tics that cause most of the problems at home. These are hard to ignore and can cause a great deal of tension for the whole family. If you want peace and quiet then a set of good old-fashioned earplugs can be a blessing.

Watching television together causes a lot of difficulties for siblings. In many cases the child with vocal tics may be sent to another room to watch television. This is unfortunate as it just adds to the feeling of low self-worth that the child probably already has. It takes him away from sharing experiences with those with whom he should feel most comfortable. If watching television together is a really big problem and it is having a major effect on the siblings and rest of the family then consider purchasing a set of dual or multi-headed headphones that plug

...g with behavioural problems

...uestion that most parents ask is: how do you know what ...urette Syndrome and what is simply defiant or naughty ...aviour? The answer is that it is extremely difficult if not ...possible. The only answer I have is that 'planned' mischief ...at is premeditated is not due to Tourette Syndrome. The ...ehavioural problems in Tourette Syndrome are usually ...impulsive and not planned.

Coprolalia is rare in children. Any rude outbursts that are a result of tics usually occur out of context, i.e. not in an argument or as part of an angry exchange and gesture. The child will also be shocked and embarrassed by it and probably apologetic.

Unless the child can verbalize why he felt the urge to carry out a particular behaviour, parents have to make a decision as to whether their child had a degree of control over it or whether it was impulsive. You know your child best so go with your instincts.

All children can be naughty, defiant, aggressive, impulsive and rude. A child with Tourette Syndrome and associated behavioural difficulties will show a lot more of the above oppositional behaviour than an average child and will therefore need more help in terms of discipline (rules and standards for acceptable behaviour) and behavioural management (learning appropriate behaviours). It is also worth noting that the more exhausting and challenging the child is, the more likely that he will receive negative and critical comments from parents and teachers. This in return will lead to a child who will develop a low self-image, be lacking in confidence and may start mixing with the 'wrong crowd' and drift into antisocial behaviour. Thus a parent of a child with Tourette Syndrome has to work extra hard to deal with the defiant child, but it will be worth it in the end.

into the television. Thus at least the child will be able to remain in the same room as his siblings.

For coprolalia (the utterance of socially unacceptable words) teach your child to say a similar-sounding, less offensive word: for example, saying 'sugar' or 'fork' for certain swear words. The same goes for unsociable motor tics. If the child has a tic that involves spitting, try getting him to change the tic to one that involves swallowing or at least getting him to spit into a tissue.

Get the child to come up with his own appropriate suggestions. Other techniques, such as habit reversal and massed practice, are mentioned in Chapter 2.

As mentioned in Chapter 2, anything that reduces stress for your child will be beneficial. That is why the time period immediately after school has finished is usually the most difficult time for parents. Children try and keep their tics controlled as much as possible during school. When they come home, they discharge their tics like 'a kettle letting off steam'. It is a credit to you and your home if your child does this, as it shows that the one place where he can be himself is home (I would be more concerned for a child if he does not feel he can relax in his own home).

Be prepared for this 'letting off steam' after school. Let your child run around and tire himself out. Alternatively, engage him in sporting activities and clubs at this time, which of course may also help his self-esteem.

In public

Many children with tics are so used to their own symptoms that they do not see any particular problem with having tics. In many ways it is other people's problem and not the child's. Dealing with members of the public and their reaction to your child's tics can cause a great deal of hurt, embarrassment, anger and sadness.

Many parents get tired of explaining or apologizing on behalf of their child. However, if you had no prior knowledge of the condition, how would you feel about a child with Tourette Syndrome who was running up and down the supermarket aisle? Most people would look disapprovingly or, if they did not show it, they would think it. Like most things in life, ignorance leads to prejudice. When out in public, remember that most people know very little about Tourette Syndrome. Thus you can choose to ignore stares and accept that people tend to look at things that are different. This is natural: we all stare at people if they are wearing something unusual, or are very thin, or fat, or from a different race or culture, or even if they have a disability. One way of coping with stares is to train yourself and your child to think that people are staring because they are curious and interested. They are looking at you because you are special!

It is when other people make a negative comment that you might want to be a bit more active. You could choose to ignore it. After all, you may never see that person again. However, many parents say that the worst thing about having a child with Tourette Syndrome is when strangers make hurtful comments. Several parents have told me that they still think about comments that were said to their child over ten years ago. It is not the comment that has upset them but the fact that they did not say anything back to the stranger and just accepted it. It is worthwhile having a set of stock phrases for replying to comments and critical stares. In fact, you could see this as an opportunity to educate the public about Tourette Syndrome! Say something such as: 'I'm sorry that you seem to be so upset, but my child cannot help coughing out loud. He has a tic disorder known as Tourette Syndrome.' If the stranger shows

some interest then you can say a b... your statement polite. If necessary be... but do not shout and get angry. Also r... you are not apologizing for your son... apologizing for the fact that the stranger r...

Teaching your child when he is a bit older... similar is also something that you might want t... him. Teaching your child to apologize after any v... involve offensive words is very important. The n... people do not mind offensive words if there is a... apology immediately afterwards.

Some children and adults carry calling cards... information on Tourette Syndrome which can also be helpful...

Be prepared

If you have a child who suffers with asthma and you decide to go out for a family hike up a hill, then you should not be surprised if your child runs into difficulties with his breathing. In the same way, with your child with motor and vocal tics, you know that he may have uncontrollable vocal outbursts, so this may cause some disruption if he was sitting in the middle of a packed audience in the theatre on a Saturday night. If you and your child are comfortable with this, then fine. However, you should not be surprised if someone complains or management ask you to move to an alternative seat. Having Tourette Syndrome does not mean you have to avoid going to the theatre. With a little planning, such as booking seats near an exit, going to a less crowded performance in the week or simply talking to the managers beforehand, you could prevent any embarrassing incidents from occurring.

Preparation

As discussed in the above section on dealing with tics, it helps to plan ahead and prevent behavioural problems from starting, or at least have in place effective strategies if they do start.

Wherever you go, be prepared to leave early. Accept that this is one of the drawbacks of having a child who is a bit more boisterous than most children. This way you will not be as emotionally upset with your child as you would have been if you had not prepared yourself. It may be disruptive for the other siblings if you are the only adult supervising and so you may have to arrange an alternative treat for them to avoid growing resentment.

There are many other ways of being prepared. If your child is going out with other children, then talk to the supervising adult beforehand. Explain that your child may have difficulties and it would be helpful if someone can look out for early signs of excitable behaviour.

If going to the cinema or theatre, choose aisle seats that enable you to make a quick exit if behaviour gets out of hand.

If going to a place where you have to wait for a long period of time, such as a restaurant or airport, make sure you have plenty of activities to distract your child. This could include books, drawing materials and pocket computer games.

Choose restaurants that serve food quickly or have a buffet service. Think about seating arrangements. It may be better to sit in between your children to stop them fighting and causing a scene.

Go to shopping malls when they are less crowded and there is less stimulation.

As above, be prepared for comments from other members of the public.

Behavioural management

The basic rule is that most children want some sort of attention. This is particularly pertinent to those children with Tourette Syndrome and associated Attention Deficit Hyperactivity Disorder (ADHD). If children do not get positive attention regularly, they will seek out negative attention, whatever that may be, and do their very best to get it.

Thus, if possible, ignore attention-seeking behaviour (unless it is dangerous or violent). If limits and boundaries are broken use strategies that are mentioned below.

Getting your child to do the things you want him to do

If carrying out a particular behaviour leads to some sort of reward (positive or negative attention) then it is more likely that the child will carry out the same behaviour again. Thus, if there is acceptable behaviour and it is rewarded with praise, the child is likely to continue it. If there is acceptable behaviour and it is not rewarded with praise, then it is likely that the behaviour will diminish. Therefore, if you want good behaviour to continue, you must keep praising and rewarding it in some small way. This can be encouraging words, pats on the back, hugs or simply saying 'I'm really proud of you'. It is a good idea to vary the praise so the child does not get bored.

Unfortunately, since children with Tourette Syndrome will be more demanding and exhausting than most, parents will find it hard to see the good behaviour and the 'naughty' behaviour dominates everyday life.

Keep a close eye on good behaviour and remember to reward it with praise if you want it to continue.

On the other hand, if there is unacceptable behaviour and you reward it with more attention than a simple verbal 'no' – maybe getting annoyed and screaming at your child – then it is likely that the behaviour will continue. If there is unacceptable behaviour and there is no reward then it is likely that the unacceptable behaviour will diminish.

For younger children (aged five to ten years), star charts and sticker books are helpful. If they accomplish a task, such as tidying their bedroom every day in the week, they get a sticker or star each day. If they have enough stickers at the end of the week they get a small treat or token. The tokens can be built up to purchase something special at the end of the month. This works best if the child has some sort of involvement such as choosing the treat or negotiating, within reason, how many stickers are needed to get a treat. To avoid this becoming monotonous, apply this to different behaviours as each behaviour improves. You should also vary the stickers and treats.

Praising your child and setting limits

Catch your child being good and praise this behaviour immediately. As seen above this will lead to the acceptable behaviour being more likely to occur. Be specific about the praise and label the behaviour that you are praising so the child clearly understands. The typical child with Tourette Syndrome will need more praise than others.

Set firm boundaries and limits. The child with Tourette Syndrome and ADHD will really test your limits and boundaries to the full. When setting limits and giving instructions:

- Be brief but clear.

- Specify the desired behaviour you want.

- Avoid trivial rules and commands. *Don't* have rules about flicking channels on the remote control. *Do* have rules about hitting. Agree with your partner on certain house rules – five or ten, not hundreds.

- Use 'when–then' commands: *when* you have tidied your bed *then* you can play.

- Praise good behaviour.

- Make sure there are consequences for not following instructions.

- Be consistent.

Believe it or not, deep down inside, children want to get praise and they want to please you! They are therefore more likely to follow instructions that are said in a positive than a negative way. For instance, if a child walks on the carpet in muddy shoes and you say 'Don't walk on the carpet with muddy shoes', the likelihood is that he will do the same next time. If you were to reframe the command and instead say 'It would be really good if you took off your muddy shoes before walking on the carpet', then a child is more likely to respond to this and take off his shoes next time.

Try this approach and you may be pleasantly surprised at the response you get.

If your child is not paying attention then make sure he can see your face. Hold him by the shoulders, look straight into his eyes and be firm with your command. It is OK to look cross but avoid shouting.

If limits are broken then try using time out, response-cost or the 1-2-3 response to back chat.

Time out
Time out should be used for serious things only, such as fighting, rudeness to you or destructive and violent behaviour.

This involves sending or taking your child to another room where he can calm down. Agree on a safe room to calm down in. Don't use the kitchen or garage where there will be sharp implements and tools. His bedroom is OK. Some parents say this does not work since their child plays with all his things in the bedroom. However, time out is exactly what it says, time out from your attention. So it should not be thought of as a punishment. Think of it as a positive way to calm down. The rule is a minute for the age of the child, so if he is eight years old he has time out for eight minutes.

Unless he is extremely violent, it is important to ignore him while in time out. He may throw things about and make a mess. If he does make a mess, make sure he is responsible for it and either tidies it up or carries out a chore to pay for any damage. Combine this with other techniques such as loss of privileges and treats.

Response-cost

This is basically the removal of privileges or payment of a fine. Many parents say their children do not seem that bothered by this, but they still persist with this as most children dislike privileges being taken away from them even if they cannot admit to it. To avoid seeming as if you are endlessly penalizing your children, counteract this with positive praise for good behaviour.

If your child has done something such as stolen sweets from a shop, make him go to the shop to apologize and pay for them. If he has damaged the neighbour's fence, then he should be made to repair it or at least do chores to pay for it. This way your child will see that he has to be responsible for his actions.

Back chat and endless arguments

Many parents often feel exhausted by the constant arguing,
'back chat' and debate they receive from their children. Once
you tell a child off, he will talk back and debate the issue
endlessly. After a few minutes you are arguing about something
completely irrelevant to what you were telling him off for in
the first place. Dr Thomas Phelan (1995) has written an
excellent book which helps deal with this when you want your
child to stop a particular behaviour. He suggests using visual
cues of raising a finger to indicate 'one', as a warning if your
child has over-stepped the boundaries. If he persists again,
which he usually will, then raise two fingers to indicate 'two'. If
he still persists then raise three fingers to indicate 'three'. The
parent should not speak at all during this, apart from saying
'one, two, three' when raising his/her respective fingers. Thus
by doing this, the parent avoids getting drawn into the
time-consuming debate which the child usually wins. With
continued use of this method, the child is likely to stop a
particular behaviour by the time you get to the first or second
stage.

A final comment

I know it is easy to say, but if at all possible try not
to lose your temper and try to stay calm. You are a
role model for your child. We tend to lose our
temper when things have been building up, when
we are not relaxed, when we are tired, hungry and
stressed. Therefore remember to look after
yourself and your health. This way, you will be in a
better frame of mind when dealing with your child.

CHAPTER SIX

Anger Management

> Anyone can become angry – that is easy. But to be angry with the right person, to the right degree, at the right time, for the right purpose and in the right way – this is not easy.
>
> *Aristotle*

Introduction

One of the most frequent questions raised by parents of children with Tourette Syndrome is: 'What can I do about my child's anger?' Aggression has a profound effect on the rest of the family and has major consequences for the child. Many of the tips mentioned in Chapter 5 help keep mild anger and behavioural problems under control.

The following chapter is really an attempt to get parents to understand anger and understand why children (and parents) get angry. This chapter contains theory on causes of anger. It then goes on to suggest ways in which anger can be explored with children and also gives a few tips on how to deal with anger. The reader is invited to use some of these techniques to manage his/her own anger.

What is anger?

Anger is what we do to protect ourselves whenever there is a threat to any of our needs. When we are threatened there are two things we can do: we can defend ourselves or we can run away. This is known as the 'fight or flight' mechanism. Anger is the choice of 'fight'. Anger is basically a way of protecting ourselves.

Why do we get angry?

The biological causes of anger include genes and hormones. Genetic factors in each individual, such as personality and temperament, make some more aggressive and angry than others.

Males tend to be naturally more aggressive than females. This is mainly due to hormones such as testosterone.

Non-biological causes for aggression include learnt behaviour and stress. We have learnt how to be angry from our parents. Parents are our role models. When we see our parents lose their temper, we copy them.

We have learnt as young children that we get things such as attention and food when we scream or make a fuss. If we don't scream or make a fuss then we do not get our way. In other words, we have learnt that anger has its benefits. So anger is sometimes used simply to get our own way.

Childhood experiences such as rejection, fears and prejudices can shape our emotions and lead to aggressive outbursts later in adolescence and adulthood.

External causes which may predispose someone to become irritable and angry include lack of sleep, lack of food (hunger), difficulties in school, poor physical health, drugs, alcohol, exams and stress.

Tourette Syndrome and aggression

As well as the above, the child with Tourette Syndrome may be impulsive, have low self-esteem and have limited capacity for flexibility and adaptability. He may think in a concrete way and cannot rationalize things as well as his peers. He may feel inflexible about certain things, such as the feel of certain clothes or the way things smell.

Try and view your child's anger outburst as a result of a lack of skills rather than a desire to get attention. He may not have the skills for flexibility and frustration tolerance. Many older adolescents talk about the feeling of 'frustration' they experienced as children and not being able to express themselves in any other way.

When a child with Tourette Syndrome is trying to suppress several tics during the day, say at school for example, he will be using up a lot of energy and this becomes exhausting for him. This will build up to a feeling of frustration and it is not uncommon for the child to be overcome with anger and have aggressive outbursts.

In between the child's angry outbursts, he is often remorseful and regrets his actions. Occasionally, some children show little remorse and may disregard other people's feelings. These children may have problems with empathy and general social skills. If this is an ongoing concern then the parent is advised to discuss this with the child's clinician.

Understand your child

Start by viewing your child differently to how you had previously done. Most parents see their children as 'little adults'; in other words, they assume that children can be reasonable, and have a good understanding of life and relationships. According to this view, if the parent explains the reasons why a child should not hit his sister or why he should not kick the furniture, the parent is assuming that the child will understand everything perfectly. This will not be the case. Remember children are not little adults. They are still children and born unreasonable and selfish – it is our job to help them.

With this new understanding of why children get angry, and also keeping in mind that they are not as wise and experienced as you, leave guilt and blame behind, realize that you are not the reason why your child is like this and start looking at solutions and re-establish better relationships. If you remain focused on understanding the child, you can relate to him better.

When dealing with conflict, try to stay calm. If you remain calm, then your child is more likely to remain calm. Occasionally, children will say hurtful things. Try not to take aggressive comments personally: if you do then you will become more stressed and more likely to lose control. If you stay in control, you show your child that it can be done and you effectively become a good role model.

Mothers tend to be at the receiving end of most children's anger. This may be because they are the ones who are usually present at home or they may be perceived as the weaker of the two parents. Avoid saying things such as 'Wait till your father comes home'. All this does is empower the father, who probably does not need to be empowered, and at the same time any authority is taken away from the mother. Parents should try and support each other when dealing with conflict.

Do not hit your child. The majority of spankings are basic parental temper tantrums. If you react violently, you will confirm your child's fears that his feelings of anger are dangerous, making it harder for him to gain control over them.

Prevention

Don't put your child in situations that will make him likely to get frustrated and angry.

When supervising children, watch for signs of increasing tension in your child and intervene early.

Limit the amount of violent television and computer games that your child watches. There is good evidence that aggressive images have an effect on children's behaviour and development.

Model flexibility and show the child how you deal with frustrations. If possible, identify feelings for him as often as you can. For example, say things such as 'That must be frustrating for you' or 'I can see that you are angry'. This gives the child the opportunity to verbally express himself appropriately.

Talking to your child about anger

It may seem obvious, but talking to your child about anger is one of the most important things you can do to help him. This should be done in a supportive way and not as a lecture or a way of blaming the child and making him feel guilty.

How many times have you said 'Why are you doing this to me?' or 'What have I done to deserve this?'? This type of language does not help the child but it reinforces the thought that your child already has that he is a naughty boy and he can influence his parents' feelings.

Teaching him about anger is important. Explain that it is OK to get angry but, as Aristotle said, 'right amount of anger with the right person, at the right time'. Anger isn't always wrong. It can be OK to be angry when we see bad things such as children starving to death, animals being treated cruelly or someone being attacked.

Teach older children that anger is really not the primary problem, but a secondary one. Anger is a reaction to a threat. The threat may be fear, embarrassment, frustration, disappointment or a range of feelings. Think about the times you have lost your temper at work or with friends. Usually it is because of some sort of threat. If the feelings behind the threat were explored further then it is likely that the anger would diminish.

For deep-seated problems and threats, one may need to consult a therapist.

Talk to your child about thoughts, emotions and actions. Behind every emotion (anger) is a thought. For instance, if your friend ignores you, you may feel angry and as a result say something rude. But before that feeling of being angry, there is the thought 'He does not like me' or 'He thinks I'm stupid'. Learning to substitute this thought is difficult but try and get your child to see that he can have alternative thoughts. A good example of how thoughts can change emotions is as follows:

Imagine you get into a lift that already has one person in it. You turn around to face the door and the lift goes up. After a few seconds you feel a sharp prod in the back. How do you feel now? What thoughts do you have? What actions would you like to take?

You choose to ignore the prod. After a few more seconds you get another sharp prod in the back. What are your thoughts and feelings now? What will you do now?

It happens again for a third time. How do you feel? Pretty annoyed? Angry? Curious? Livid? Remember this feeling.

Now you have had enough and you turn around.

You see a man in dark glasses and a white stick. How do you feel now? Embarrassed? Guilty? Concerned?

This example demonstrates how powerful thoughts are over feelings. If we can focus on our thoughts, then we can start to understand some of the feelings and in turn aim to address the thoughts.

For instance, in the situation above, your friend ignores you. You may come up with the thought 'He is daydreaming' or 'He has a lot on his mind'. Obviously, if he ignores you and tells you he is deliberately ignoring you, then that's different and you have every right to be angry. Try and come up with non-angry thoughts. This is not easy but give it a go. If we can control the way we think, then this controls the way we feel.

Explain the cost of anger so the child understands that anger does not just get the child in trouble. It has an effect on friendship and relationships; it can affect finances, self-esteem and school work; and it can lead to having a criminal record. It also leads to attacks on the body such as stomach ulcers, heart problems and hypertension.

Tips for dealing with anger

- Count to a hundred.

- Draw a picture.

- Drink water or juice.

- Write down your thoughts.

- Write down funny jokes.

- Move away.

- Listen to music.

- Take a bath.

- It may be helpful to keep an anger diary.

- Use humour to minimize the threat.

Express anger appropriately

As mentioned above, it is OK to be angry but there are ways of expressing the same feeling more effectively than by shouting at someone. Before speaking to the other person try to relax by releasing the tension that has been building up. Do this by talking to yourself. It also helps to avoid getting into a confrontational stance, so step back and pause. Try and remain calm and check your breathing. Breathe slowly. Now you are more relaxed and ready to speak. Express feelings, and suggest solutions.

If possible when expressing yourself, don't blame, do not be rude, do not be confrontational and do not exaggerate.

After an incident make time to talk to the child about feelings. Do not do this straight away when the situation is still tense. Wait for a convenient time later in the day or the next day.

If anger is a really major issue and dominating your and your child's lives, then expert advice is probably needed. As mentioned above, in many cases there are deep emotional issues behind the anger and it may be better if a neutral person talks to the child.

A psychologist or school counsellor can help. There may be anger management courses locally. For most anger management courses, the child has to have a reasonable degree of motivation if there is to be a reasonable chance of success.

If anger persists then it may be worth discussing this with the child's clinician who may consider prescribing medication in extreme cases.

CHAPTER SEVEN

Educational Issues

Introduction

If you can create the right environment for teaching and understanding in school, the child with Tourette Syndrome will flourish and grow in confidence. Educational issues are likely to have much more of an impact on prognosis than any medicines or psychological therapies. If educational issues are not addressed, then the potential for bullying, developing poor social skills, academic underachievement and low self-esteem is high.

Once a diagnosis is made, parents are often faced with the decision of whether the school should be aware of the problem or not. On the one hand, the parent is protective of the child and does want to give him a label with a stigma attached which may hamper his progress at school. The label itself may undermine the child's confidence if it is not handled sensitively, since no child really wants to be considered different from his classmates.

On the other hand, if the child is suffering emotionally, physically and academically, then it is usually in his best interests for the school to be informed. Yes, there is a lot of stigma still around, but things are changing as more people become aware of the condition.

Parent–teacher relationship

Teachers find it helpful if they are told in advance the problems they may face with a child. It is a good idea to have a meeting prior to the start of each new school year. Although teachers can pass information from one year to the next, a face-to-face meeting makes it personal and actively involves the teacher.

Let teachers know what medication the child is on. It is a good idea to give permission for the prescribing doctor to write a brief note to the school every time there is a change with medication. Teachers need to know about certain side-effects of medicines such as drowsiness, school phobia and anxiety.

Teachers can be useful clinically since they are in a good position to monitor progress. A teacher's report on issues such as social skills and peer relationships is also often helpful.

When meeting teachers, have handouts available which contain the basic facts on Tourette Syndrome. Give out information on training days or relevant articles (these bits of information are also useful for local doctors).

Have action plans ready if things go wrong (it amazes me why teachers continue to phone up parents just to simply say their child has just been naughty in class – what do they expect the parents to do?!). Agree on rules, thus making a consistent home–school programme. Volunteer to help on outings.

Be constructive and avoid arguments: remember, not everyone deals with things in the same way. Make sure schools can contact you in case of emergencies.

Above all be open and honest and keep the line of communication open.

What the teacher needs to know

As mentioned in Chapter 1, there is a wide range of tics that a child can present with. It is therefore extremely important that the teachers are aware of not only the symptoms but also the nature of the tics. The teachers specifically need to know that the child has little control over the tics and is not doing it on purpose or 'to get attention'. It is a sad but realistic thought that every day there will be a child with a tic disorder in a classroom somewhere who will be reprimanded for his tics. It is not uncommon to hear about children given detentions or extra homework because the teacher assumes the tics are done deliberately to annoy him/her.

A teacher who is knowledgeable about tic disorders can help reduce the stress for the child in the classroom by ignoring the mild tics. In return this should make the child feel more comfortable and, as a result, may reduce the frequency and intensity of the tics. The teacher is the role model in the classroom and thus, if the teacher accepts the tics, it is likely that the pupils will do the same.

The teacher should be aware that stress could precipitate tics. Exam time is particularly difficult (see below) as is any oral performance such as reciting in front of the class or school. Having said this, it is difficult to get the balance right as to what one should do about performing in public. If the child is worried about speaking in public because of his tics, then making him the centre of attention is not going to help. On the other hand, avoidance of normal school experiences may reinforce phobias and the child may feel he is missing out. The best solution is for the teacher to talk to the child in private beforehand and ask what he wants to do. Remember that there are many actors and politicians out there with tics who would not have made a career of acting or politics if they were held back when it came to public performances at school.

Depending on how the child and parents feel, it is sometimes a good idea for other pupils to learn about tics. If the child with Tourette Syndrome feels confident enough, it might be empowering if he could give a short presentation to the class on Tourette Syndrome and describe what it is like to have the condition. This can be done in a personal development lesson, a general studies lesson or even a science lesson.

Problems and interventions

Tics

The general rule for dealing with motor and vocal tics in school is to ignore them.

If the tics are particularly noisy or troublesome, then it is often helpful for the child to know that he can leave the classroom and go to the nurse's office, the toilets or another quiet place. Although most children with Tourette Syndrome admit to suppressing their tics during lessons, this is not necessarily a good idea as the child often puts all his energy into holding back the tic. Consequently, his concentration and attention are affected and may not be performing to his abilities. It is important that the school teachers are aware that during a bad phase of troublesome tics, academic performance may be down.

If the child is going through a particularly bad spell of tics then it might be in his best interests to have permission for frequent breaks from the classroom. This may include frequent visits to the toilet, or being given errands around the school. Teachers could agree that when the tics are increasing in severity, the child can be given a sealed envelope to deliver to another teacher in another part of the school, thus having an excuse to leave the classroom and 'release' the tics.

Obsessive Compulsive Disorder

As mentioned in Chapter 3, some children with Tourette Syndrome may also have co-existing Obsessive Compulsive Disorder (OCD). This may present itself in the classroom in a variety of ways. The child may need to count out to himself during lessons, re-read things over again or rewrite letters until they are perfect. Obviously, this may have a profound effect on concentration as well as being extremely time consuming. Children with OCD should be given the option of having extra time for assignments as well as help and support in exams.

Attention Deficit Hyperactivity Disorder

Research has shown that when a child with Tourette Syndrome is having major difficulties in the classroom, it is usually because he has co-existing Attention Deficit Hyperactivity Disorder (ADHD). The knowledge of various classroom strategies for dealing with symptoms of ADHD is thus important to the teacher.

A simple method of dealing with specific hyperactive behaviour in the classroom is to move the child's desk away from a child with similar hyperactive symptoms and place him closer to the teacher. This reduces possible disruptive behaviour and gives the teacher a better opportunity to monitor behaviour and give positive feedback. Moving the child's desk away from the window will also reduce possible distractions.

Hyperactive children need a lot more routine and clear, simple classroom rules than most children. Scheduling structured tasks before unstructured tasks reduces the difficulties hyperactive children have in changing activities and settling down to work. Thus, if possible, arranging the daily classroom activities in such a way that formal tasks like reading come before informal tasks like painting or drama may be more productive.

Hyperactive children respond well to positive praise and encouragement. Occasionally the child may need more encouragement than simply verbal comments. 'Token programmes' are a useful visual way of showing praise for achievement. Token programmes allow the child to collect tokens such as stickers and stars for good behaviour and exchange them at the end of the day or week for privileges. Of course, any chosen programme should ideally use tokens and rewards that appeal to the individual child. Token programmes are often useful for the whole class and prevent the spotlight being placed on the child with ADHD.

Use of a good behaviour diary, in which the teacher can put a tick next to a number of appropriate behaviours such as staying in his seat, finishing a task, or completing work, is often helpful. This also allows the child and parent to see and monitor progress.

In combination with frequent positive praise and encouragement, negative responses, such as ignoring and time out, are also needed to reinforce the fact that certain behaviours such as aggression are unacceptable.

The teacher needs to be aware that concentration and attention is a major problem for these children. The teacher should not be surprised to see that the young Ryan, who has ADHD, has already started playing up ten minutes into the quiet reading lesson. Providing a bit more structure to these lessons will make the child feel more contained and able to concentrate.

If the teacher breaks down projects into smaller assignments over a short period of time, the child with ADHD is more likely to stay on task and complete the work. For instance, if a child has one term to complete and hand in a geography project, break the project down into smaller parts to be done in weekly instalments: the background reading needs to be done by Week 1, the introduction needs to be written up by Week 2, the method written up by Week 3, etc.

The child with ADHD will often lose things. While missing school work needs to be taken seriously, the teacher should avoid penalizing the child who constantly forgets small items such as pens or paper. It may be helpful for the teacher to have a spare supply of pens and pencils for the child who constantly loses these items.

Work presentation

The teacher should:

- break work down in small chunks

- use visual cues as much as possible

- allow the use of a dictaphone

- allow the child to photocopy someone else's notes.

Maths

Again, the teacher should break down the work into small chunks and provide fewer problems on each worksheet. Thus, instead of 20 questions to be done in 20 minutes, the teacher should give the child one individual question to be done in one minute, then move on to Question 2, and so on.

If the actual writing of numbers is a particular problem, allow the use of graph paper to keep numbers within small cells.

Classroom environment

This follows similar guidance for children who have ADHD. The teacher should sit the child with Tourette Syndrome away from distractions, in a place where he has space to release his tics, such as the side of a classroom or near the door if he needs to make a quick exit. Avoid seating him in the middle of the class or directly at the front where the whole class can see him. Remember that many children with Tourette Syndrome can feel claustrophobic in small rooms.

Grading

The teacher should allow the pupil with Tourette Syndrome extra time to complete his work.

If his handwriting and organization are particularly bad, give him separate marks for content and presentation.

Allow use of a word processor for writing up projects.

If the child consistently gets poor marks, mark only if he scores a correct answer. Seeing red crosses every day on one's work can be demoralizing. Continuous praise should be given for effort.

Handwriting

If the child's handwriting is particularly poor, the teacher should allow him to use a word processor. Alternatively, utilizing something simple such as graph paper will make sure letters and digits fit in cells.

Enquire as to whether certain aids for holding pens and pencils will be helpful. This is usually done through the occupational therapy services but the Special Educational Needs Coordinator (SENCO) may be able to advise.

Use worksheets that require minimum handwriting.

Provide a printout of any details written on the blackboard for children who find it difficult copying things quickly from the blackboard. Nowadays many schools provide white boards that automatically produce printouts of what has been written on them.

The teacher could also allow the child to tape the lesson on a dictaphone if he cannot copy things quickly.

Homework

For many children with Tourette Syndrome, the last thing they want to do at the end of a stressful day at school is homework. The child usually feels tired as well as unmotivated. If homework has to be done, then there are some ways of making it less unpleasant for the child.

As mentioned above, teachers should break the work into small chunks and recognize that not all of the work will get done.

Parents could use homework diaries to organize the pupil. Make sure the teacher of each lesson has seen that the required homework has been written down in the diary. This avoids the child 'forgetting' to write it down. Parents could check this with teachers or with other pupils' parents.

Another simple way to make sure homework is done is for the teacher to allow the pupil to do the homework for the morning lessons during the lunch break. This can be done in the library or a selected classroom. This is particularly effective for those children who are easily distracted by siblings at home. It also helps keep the child out of trouble during the unstructured lunch break at school. Many children with associated ADHD take stimulant medication to help with concentration. These medicines have side-effects such as insomnia and hence pupils are advised not to take the medicine later than the afternoon. Thus the work produced in the morning and afternoon will be very different from the work produced in the evening when the effect of medication has worn off. This is another good reason to allow the child to do homework at break periods during school time.

USEFUL TIPS FOR PARENTS ON HOW TO APPROACH HOMEWORK

- Decide when the best time is for your child to do his homework (some children like to relax first; others like to start when they get home from school).

- Identify a place away from open distractions (some children like to have some background noise; others prefer quiet). Avoid clutter on desk surfaces.

- Check your child's homework schedule.

- Plan the homework and decide what homework can be realistically done that evening.

- What information and equipment does your child need to get started?

- It's often helpful to choose a reward your child can look forward to when the homework has finished, such as watching TV or playing a game. Remember, TV programmes can be recorded so your child can see them after he has finished his homework.

Motivation

Many experienced teachers say that the major obstacle to learning is fear. This could be fear of failure, fear of criticism or fear of appearing stupid. If schools are able to remove fear then pupils will at least try and learn. The child should feel able to make mistakes and learn from them.

Setting realistic goals is important for motivation. Teachers should negotiate specific targets with the pupil.

Focus on the pupil's strengths instead of always highlighting his weaknesses.

Give continuous support.

Allow for extra time for certain projects or deadlines.

Make subjects interesting for the child. For example, when learning capital cities of Europe in a geography lesson, get the soccer-mad pupil to tell you about relevant European soccer teams.

Exams

It will be easier to implement changes for exams that are organized internally by schools than for exams organized by external examination boards. However, many examination boards are understanding and, with a bit of planning, changes can be made.

Usually examination boards allow the child's usual method of working in the classroom to be continued in the examination hall. So if he uses a lap-top in a particular lesson, then he should be allowed to use the lap-top in that particular exam. The important thing for parents to remember is to submit applications for special arrangements for exams as early as possible with supportive letters from teachers and specialists involved such as psychologists and doctors.

Modifications for children with Tourette Syndrome include allowing extra time to take tests, providing movement and breaks during exams, allowing the test to be read to the child, allowing the child to respond verbally and allowing the use of a word processor.

Recess, lunchtime and transition from lesson to lesson

Recess and transferring from lesson to lesson are not only very noisy but are also less supervised by teachers. It is therefore not uncommon to hear that little Connor, who has Tourette Syndrome, behaves well in class but gets into fights during recess. Possible interventions include alerting the child a few minutes earlier to the fact that there will be a classroom change, allowing the child to leave the classroom two or three minutes early to avoid crowded corridors or making sure there is a teacher nearby during lunch breaks to prevent possible confrontations.

Some children with co-existing ADHD may take methylphenidate (Ritalin) medication at morning and lunchtimes. If it is particularly difficult for the child to stay out of trouble during lunchtime, then consideration needs to be given to taking the lunchtime dose of medication slightly earlier, before the lunch break. This must be agreed on with the child's doctor as stimulant medication may suppress appetite, resulting in a child avoiding his lunch.

Aggression, short fuse and oppositional behaviour difficulties

Children with Tourette Syndrome are easily frustrated. They have a disorder that prevents them from keeping still for long. They may also be in pain because of certain tics. They may be stimulated by crowds of people, such as in the classroom, but also in unstructured settings, such as recess and going from lesson to lesson. All this needs to be taken into consideration when dealing with a child who presents with oppositional behaviour or loses his temper easily. The teacher may have to treat the child with Tourette Syndrome differently to his classmates and ignore minor behaviours that are not too disruptive.

The child should be taught strategies for releasing appropriate aggression (see Chapter 6). Interventions must focus on helping the child understand that, although it is difficult to control aggressive urges and impulses, aggression in school is unacceptable and appropriate strategies for releasing anger should be learnt. These include allowing him to relax or withdraw to a safe place to calm down. Having a room with a pillow or punch bag for releasing aggression is often helpful for the aggressive and agitated child.

Teaching the child to 'make a graceful exit' prior to a build-up of aggression can be effective at preventing incidents in the classroom. Often the child will not be in the right frame of mind to ask if he can leave. Therefore, a private agreement that the child can leave the classroom should he get overwhelmed may also diffuse any potential aggressive outbursts. If the child is able to divert his anger, the child should be praised for using alternative methods of releasing anger.

The teacher should be helped to recognize the signs of impending loss of control. These signs could include increased activity levels, a change in facial expression, the exacerbation of tics or increased anxiety. The teacher could then agree a set of visual or auditory cues or gestures with the child so that when the teacher notices that loss of control is imminent, the child is shown the cue and allowed to leave the room. It is always helpful for the teacher to talk to the child about outbursts only after the child has calmed down and is feeling relaxed. Once again, the child should be rewarded with praise for leaving the classroom before an incident has been allowed to develop.

Social skills

The teacher should lead by example by ignoring the tics and not criticizing the child. The teacher can make frequent reminders for making good eye contact and other basic social skills.

Role play involving games that include turn-taking and talking and responding appropriately to others are also helpful.

Talking about feelings and discussing the impact of certain behaviours on those around him can be revealing for the child.

Some schools use various methods and programmes for helping children who lack confidence and have difficulties making friends. One such programme, which is popular in the UK, is known as Circle of Friends. The object of this programme is to make sure that the child who has difficulties with friendships is included in activities and made to feel part of the group. A facilitator is required and is usually a teacher or SENCO. A social 'map' is prepared for the child, with the child's help, consisting of his social contacts. Concentric circles are drawn. In the centre is the child. In the next ring are his closest support people, such as parents and siblings. In the next circle are his advocates, such as teachers, counsellor and doctor. In the outer circle are his friends. Usually this circle has the fewest people. Volunteers are asked to be in the child's circles and act as mentors for the child. These classmates make sure they greet the child, play with him at recess and are generally helpful. They also include him in activities. There are weekly meetings in which the mentors talk about good things that have happened in the week and also discuss problem areas and how things could improve. The child also participates and tells what he liked and did not like that week. The goal is a situation in which everyone learns and friendships develop.

Use of computers

Many children with Tourette Syndrome also have problems with writing, holding a pen and looking up at the blackboard and copying things down. If a child is constantly criticized for poor handwriting, which he simply cannot help, it can have a devastating effect on a child's self-esteem.

We now live in a computer age and almost every workplace or industry relies on computers in some form. This is good news for the child who might have problems with writing and visuo-motor coordination. The computer makes writing and coordination a lot easier. It also contains spell checks and helps with grammar. Thus if a child with Tourette Syndrome also has fine motor coordination difficulties, then he should be allowed to use a word processor for some academic work. Access to a lap-top in class would greatly help a child who is struggling with a pen and paper.

Sleep hygiene

A tired child is not going to concentrate in school. It is therefore important that the child with Tourette Syndrome has a good night's sleep before school days. Try and establish a bedtime routine of going to bed at a set time and waking up at the same time every morning. Avoid eating late and watching television late in the evenings.

Statement and resources

Every school should have a policy to make sure that all children reach their academic potential. Most children's educational needs will be met by the mainstream school system. If a child has special educational needs then this must be recognized and appropriate measures must be taken to help the child. If the school is unable to provide help then schools should apply for resources for that particular child. The help needed may be supplying specific reading material, use of a lap-top or providing a support teacher for several hours during the week.

In the UK, the process of getting help is called 'statementing'. There are five stages to getting a Statement of Special Educational Needs (Department for Education 1994):

- *Stage 1.* The class teacher identifies difficulties, discusses it with parents and informs the school's SENCO. Intervention is managed by the class teacher.

- *Stage 2.* If difficulties continue, then an Individual Educational Plan (IEP) is drawn up. The plan will set targets for the child to achieve and a date for a review to see what progress he has made.

- *Stage 3.* The school may now involve specialist services for advice. The educational psychologist or specialist teacher is asked to assess the child and give appropriate advice.

- *Stage 4.* The Local Educational Authority (LEA) is asked to make a statutory assessment. This is a detailed examination to find out about a child's educational needs. The LEA will look at detailed assessments carried out by the educational psychologist and other reports from professionals. The LEA then considers whether a Statement of Special Educational Needs should be issued. A Statement of Special Educational Needs is a document that sets out a child's needs and all the special help he should have. The LEA will issue a Statement when they decide that all the special help a child needs cannot reasonably be provided within the resources normally available to the school.

- *Stage 5.* If appropriate, the LEA issues a Statement of Special Educational Needs. Regular review dates will be set to monitor progress.

CHAPTER EIGHT

Dealing with Bullying

Introduction

Most people have encountered some form of bullying in their lives. No one is immune from it and many A-list celebrities such as Tom Cruise, Harrison Ford and Michele Pfeiffer have all been victims of bullying in the past.

Bullying can have significant and long-term adverse effects on the health and behaviour of children. It is therefore imperative that it is taken seriously. If your child is in any way different from others, perhaps having a different accent, different skin colour or a mental or physical disability, or even simply behaving differently, then at some stage someone is likely to make a negative comment and, if this continues, your child may become a victim of bullying. In some cases bullying occurs even if there are no differences.

The child with tics is different from the majority of children in his class. He may stand out because of unusual motor tics and loud vocal tics or because of associated behaviours such as impulsivity, poor handwriting and academic difficulties. Other children in the classroom may see these differences as a chance to poke fun and tease the child. It is therefore important that all parents of children with Tourette

Syndrome be prepared to deal with the difficult and emotional issues of bullying.

A definition of bullying

Bullying occurs when a person is exposed repeatedly to negative actions on the part of one or more other persons. A negative action is when someone intentionally inflicts, or attempts to inflict, some form of injury. It also occurs when there is an unequal power relationship between the bully and the victim (Olweus 1994). This distinguishes bullying from the playground fight between two children of equal power.

Bullying can be direct or indirect. Direct bullying consists of physical aggression, name-calling and unpleasant gestures. Indirect bullying involves ignoring or isolating a child and spreading rumours about him.

Long-term effects of bullying

Bullying is unpleasant and unfair, and it can have a profound and lasting effect on a child. The child may experience emotional difficulties such as nightmares or anxiety and, in some cases, the bullying may lead directly to the development of major psychiatric disorders such as depression, anxiety or post-traumatic stress disorder. It may lead to problems at school, problems with relationships and self-harm or even suicide.

Victims of bullying

Children who are prone to being picked on are often said to have the following characteristics:

- an anxious and sensitive personality

- low self-esteem

- a loner with very few friends

- passive and easily dominated

- experiencing being bullied at home.

However, in some cases it may be just bad luck and the child just happens to be 'in the wrong place at the wrong time'. Nevertheless, it is useful for parents and professionals to recognize the above characteristics and keep in mind that such a child is vulnerable to being bullied.

Characteristics of typical bullies

Bullies tend to:

- be aggressive towards peers and adults

- often not be as popular as others, surrounded by a small peer group of two or three other children

- have a psychological need for power

- have been bullied by others

- have experienced family problems

- feel insecure and unimportant – bullying gives them power

- be unable to understand how their victim feels; in other words, they cannot empathize with others

- be envious of others.

Bullying and Tourette Syndrome

Of course, being different in any way whatsoever is a sure sign that one may get picked on. Having tics unfortunately means being slightly different from the majority; thus the likelihood that your child with tics will be bullied is extremely high.

Another reason why children with Tourette Syndrome are picked on is that they have the characteristics of 'provocative victims': they have a combination of both anxious and aggressive reaction patterns. Children with Tourette Syndrome may have problems with concentration and be impulsive. They may have associated features of Attention Deficit Hyperactivity Disorder (ADHD) and be hyperactive and fidgety. Their behaviour may cause irritation and tension around themselves. This will annoy many of their classroom peer group. Other children may decide actively to avoid the child with tics 'in case they catch a dreaded disease' and they may also make fun of him.

Children with Tourette Syndrome and associated impulsive traits often have major aggressive outbursts and are easily wound up. Other children will be quick to see this and do their best to wind up the child and get him into trouble.

Taking the above into consideration it is important that you and your child are prepared for this. Some of the tips mentioned in Chapter 9 will be helpful in preventing any name-calling from having a profound, detrimental effect. Professionals also have a role to play in enquiring about bullying and in some cases writing helpful letters of support to the school regarding possible bullying.

Recognizing the signs of bullying

Signs that your child is being bullied include:

- withdrawal

- becoming argumentative

- developing school phobia

- having academic problems

- stealing

- sleeping badly

- wetting and soiling the bed

- having injuries

- experiencing low self-esteem

- regressing

- feeling depressed

- missing possessions.

Parents of children with Tourette Syndrome are often aware that their child may be a bit disorganized and frequently loses things. This is often due to poor memory or poor concentration. However, one needs to keep in mind that if valuable or favourite items go missing – maybe trading cards, dinner money or trendy bags and clothes – ask the child what has happened to them. Other children may have stolen them. Alternatively, the child may be giving these items to a bully in order to placate him and stay on his good side.

What to do if your child is being bullied

It is important that your child knows that you are taking this seriously. Listen to your child, establish the sequence of events and get the facts as accurate as possible. Your child needs to be reassured that you will do all you can to stop the bullying. He also needs you to stay calm and in control and the last thing he wants is you saying you are going round to the school to 'teach the bully a lesson'. Explain that you and his class teacher will try to tackle this. Do not agree to keep the bullying a secret, but explain that the bully is probably hurting other children and thus you and your child will be protecting them as well.

Once you have the facts, arrange to see the class teacher as soon as possible. Some parents prefer to go directly to the head teacher straight away. This may be appropriate if the bully is in another class to your child. However, if the bully is in the same class, then talking to the head teacher in the first instance may undermine the class teacher's abilities to deal with the bully.

When you meet with the class teacher, ask him or her to investigate the matter and to keep you informed. Ask about the school anti-bullying policy and that you expect to receive an update. This ensures that the teacher does not just pay you lip service and that there will be some sort of follow-up.

It is a good idea to make notes at the time of the meeting or immediately afterwards. Keep a record of all meetings. Also keep a diary of all reported bullying incidents including dates and injuries.

You should expect the school to treat bullying incidents seriously. Teachers should do what they can to protect your child. Interviews need to be conducted with the victim, bully or bullies, witnesses and parents of both parties. The bully should be given an opportunity to express him- or herself but also he or she needs to see that his or her behaviour is unacceptable. Some sort of action should be taken against the bully. The following are measures that can be taken by schools:

- making the bully apologise, face to face or with a written apology

- getting the bully to perform some sort of service for the class and school such as cleaning out the school fish tank or picking up litter in the playground

- putting the bully in detention after school or keeping him or her in at lunchtimes.

If the bullying continues or if the incident is particularly severe, perhaps involving weapons, then the school should consider exclusion.

If you feel your child's school is not taking your concerns seriously enough and you have spoken to the head teacher, then talk to the school parent–teachers' association and school governors.

Helping your child deal with bullies

As mentioned above, low self-esteem is a risk factor for becoming a victim of bullying. Thus anything that you can do to help raise your child's self-esteem is helpful (see Chapter 9).

Once you are aware that your child is being bullied, talk to him about why people bully. Understanding why someone bullies helps the victim start to think about ways of coping and dealing with insults. Talk about your own experiences and memories. This helps the child see that he is not alone and that you have an understanding of what he may be going through.

Coping with taunts

The best way to deal with name-calling is to ignore it. Bullies are expecting an angry reaction and thus will be taken aback if there is no response.

Helping your child turn insults into compliments is useful and he can be as creative as he wants. For example, if someone says 'Hey, Ticcy, you are a bag of nerves', then an appropriate response would be 'Yes, you are correct, I do consist of nerves'. Agreeing with a bully is a great way of diffusing a situation.

Often, if a class has a child with tics, it is not unusual for other children to mimic the tics. If this occurs, your child can use the same technique and he can say something similar such as 'Hey, imitation is a form of flattery – thank you'. This confuses the bully and gives the victim a bit of control. As a parent you can practise these comments and replies with your child and also take part in some role-playing with him.

Getting your child to express his feelings may sometimes be useful if bullying continues. If someone calls your child names, then simply saying 'you should not say things like that' is unlikely to stop the bully. In fact using the word 'should' is more likely to encourage the bully to continue. If your child were to say 'I get upset when you say those words' without sounding like a victim, the bully again will be stopped in his tracks and slightly surprised.

Taking precautions

Make sure your child avoids putting himself in situations where the bully can pick on him. This may involve avoiding parts of the playground or changing the route to school. If bullying occurs at lunchtime, encourage your child to take up a lunchtime activity that will keep him indoors, such as chess or going to the library.

Other support

If your child is having difficulty coping, then ask around to see if there are any local support groups for victims of bullying. Social services, child and adolescent mental health services or volunteers' organizations may arrange these groups.

If you feel your child is having nightmares, panic attacks, school phobia or depression then talk to your doctor who may then make a referral to your local child and family mental health service.

What schools can do to discourage bullying

Most schools in the UK should have some form of anti-bullying policy. However, as teachers are extremely busy professionals, some of them may need to be reminded that they have an anti-bullying policy and that bullying is happening in their classroom. Parents can ask for a copy of the anti-bullying policy from their school head teachers or local education authority.

The ideal school should foster an environment in which any pupil that is being bullied or who witnesses bullying is encouraged to talk to teachers about it. Some schools have 'bully boxes' where pupils can put in notes about bullying. Other schools have regular meetings about bullying in the classroom as part of the core student curriculum.

Professor Dan Olweus, an expert in dealing with bullying, showed that relatively simple interventions that raise awareness of bullying behaviour in schools and set standards that promote social behaviour can have a significant effect on rates of bullying (Olweus 1994). His programmes in Bergen, Norway, led to schools developing policies that included:

- regular class meetings to enforce rules of anti-bullying policy

- the development of effective methods for reporting bullying

- shared responsibility for bullying that includes the whole class

- raising awareness of bullying by the use of questionnaires

- school conference days on the implications of bullying.

How to prevent your child from becoming a bully

Although parents are upset and shocked when they first realize that their child is being bullied, equally they may be distraught if they realize their own child is the classroom bully. As mentioned above, bullies have certain characteristics. In some cases the child with Tourette Syndrome may be the next potential candidate for the role of classroom bully. He may have felt picked on by others, but if he is also impulsive or has features of associated ADHD, he may release his aggression on others.

Sometimes the home environment can shape whether children become bullies. The following are family factors that can predispose someone to becoming a bully (Olweus 1994):

1. The basic emotional attitude of the primary caretaker(s) (usually the mother) towards the child during the early years. A negative emotional attitude, characterized by lack of warmth and

involvement, increases the likelihood that the child will be aggressive and hostile.

2. Permissiveness towards aggressive behaviour by the child. If the primary carer is generally permissive and tolerant, without setting clear limits on aggressive behaviours towards peers, siblings and adults, the child's aggression level is likely to increase.

3. Use of power-assertive child-rearing methods such as physical punishment and violent emotional outbursts. Children of parents who make frequent use of these methods are likely to become more aggressive than the average child.

Professionals who encounter families with the above characteristics may want to think about talking to the parents about their parenting style and the possible effect on the children. Help may be sought through referral to parent training groups or child and adolescent mental health services.

Teaching acceptable behaviour

Most of the preventative work on behaviour should be done at home during the child's early years. By the time they start school, children should have some reasonable control on their aggression.

Parents have an important role to play and need to:

- set an example of good relationships

- show that conflict and disagreement can take place without aggression

- teach the child that violent behaviour is unacceptable

- teach caring and empathic relationships

- show how the victim may feel

- encourage the child to talk about feelings if upset and angry.

A lot of the above involves teaching and thus parents need to be active as it is no good relying on the hope that the child may one day grow out of his aggression.

Dealing with anger and aggression

Managing anger is mainly covered in Chapter 6; however, preventative work can start early by helping your child channel aggression into sports or other activities. This also has an effect on self-esteem, and low self-esteem is another contributing factor in shaping a bully.

Supervision

Parents and professionals assume that all children are the same and require the same level of supervision to prevent aggression. This is clearly not the case and however time-consuming and impractical it may be, if your child has a history of impulsive aggressive acts, you should not be surprised to find that there has been yet another 'incident' when he was left unsupervised for half an hour with his mates.

The issue of supervision is equally important in schools as bullying tends to be worse when normal supervision is at its lowest. Recess and lunchtimes are obvious times when an aggressive child is likely to bully others. Thus, if possible, schools should provide more supervision during these times. This not only protects the victims but also helps the aggressive child.

CHAPTER NINE

Ways to Improve Your Child's Self-Esteem

Introduction

'Self-esteem' is defined as basically how we feel about ourselves most of the time. People with high self-esteem generally feel good about themselves the majority of the time. They are usually confident, outgoing and fairly sociable people. People with low self-esteem feel bad about themselves the majority of the time. They may not feel as good, clever or attractive as others. They often feel others are better and as a result they tend to withdraw from taking part in things, including social events. This feeling about oneself usually starts in childhood and is built on over many years.

Some people may be genetically predisposed to developing a form of low self-esteem, particularly if there is a history of clinical depression in the family. These people have a pessimistic outlook on life, including their abilities to achieve things and how others view them.

For the majority of people, the message that children feel they are not worthy or not any good usually comes from parents, family members, other children and occasionally teachers. These people shape a child's view of himself, as they are the people the child looks up to for guidance and approval. Many people reading this chapter can readily recall a certain negative comment that may have been made by parents and teachers ten, twenty, thirty or more years ago. They can still remember how they felt when the comment was made and the impact on their emotions. It is interesting that we are not so good at recalling so actively the positive comments said to us during our childhood.

Most people have had to deal with occasional negative comments in their life and can be hurt and upset by them, but usually the emotional effect does not dominate their life and cause serious impairment. Occasional negative comments can spur a child on to achieving great things if only in order to prove the parent or teacher that they were wrong with their comments. If the negative comments are not just 'one-offs', tend to occur on most days and are delivered by a range of people about a range of issues, then it is easy to see how the young child will start to develop a sense of poor self-image and self-worth.

Tourette Syndrome and self-esteem

The child with Tourette Syndrome may have low self-esteem for a number of reasons. He may be criticized by parents, siblings and other members of the family for making noises or fidgeting. These are things that he simply cannot control and are a part of him. He will be told off for these 'habits' and although he may protest that he cannot help making noises or sudden movements, he may not be believed by everyone. If he is told that he is a 'naughty' person enough times, he might start believing he really is one.

He may be ridiculed in school by his classmates and be the victim of physical bullying. He may even be punished by teachers because of his motor and vocal tics. The teacher may assume that the child's vocal tic or echolalia is a form of disobedience and that it is deliberately done to be disruptive to the whole class. This may result in the child being unfairly punished in front of his peers. If this continues it will have a devastating effect on the child's self-esteem. In addition, the child with Tourette Syndrome may also have academic problems due to associated features of Attention Deficit Hyperactivity Disorder (ADHD). He may have concentration difficulties or poor handwriting. He may also be clumsy at certain sports due to coordination difficulties. All of these things may lead to criticism from the teachers or his peers. The child himself will feel bad: no one wants to feel as if he is academically behind his peers in the classroom.

It is likely that the child with Tourette Syndrome may not be praised as much as his peers in school and may even be unfairly criticized. This would lead to the child feeling that he is not as good as his peers. Thus it is not surprising to see that the child with Tourette Syndrome is extremely vulnerable to developing low self-esteem.

Here is a measure of just how important self-esteem is: many children with a severe form of Tourette Syndrome that involves loud vocal tics or obvious, painful motor jerks can still feel confident about themselves so long as they have had supportive peer groups, parents and teachers. The outlook and prognosis for that child is likely to be good since the child will accept who he is and be content with his own abilities. He will recognize his own weaknesses but at the same time also recognize his own strengths. This will be mainly due to the attitude of his family and peer group, who accept that the 'annoying' loud noises that the child suddenly makes are part of his condition and cannot be helped. His friends and family are not constantly on his back telling him to stop making noises or giving him 'critical looks'. The child grows up feeling confident about his abilities and accepts that having Tourette Syndrome makes him slightly different from others but not that much different.

On the other hand, the child with relatively minor tics, such as blinking or occasional mild neck twitches, may be devastated by these tics if his surrounding peer group and family are not supportive. His parents may constantly criticize him for his habit of blinking or movement of the neck. Thus not only is life in school a difficult time because of bullying and being told off by teachers, but life at home, which is supposed to be an escape from the pressures of school, is equally hostile and difficult. The child has no allies or support and is likely to withdraw into himself. With no support the child will feel worthless and may develop depression or even thoughts of self-harm. Thus the way a child views himself and his tics is vitally important for a healthier outlook.

Helping to build up the self-esteem of children with Tourette Syndrome should not be overlooked when thinking about management issues.

Improving self-esteem

Continuous praise

Children need to know that their parents love them and have faith in them regardless of their abilities. Even in infancy, the use of praise for walking those first few steps or putting one Lego brick onto another will be registered by the infant in some way and will encourage him to repeat the act. The child will build on his efforts but will look to his parents for approval. All children want to please their parents and get a positive response. It makes them feel secure and confident. As the child develops, he looks towards his parents for some sort of feedback. This even continues into adulthood.

If parents are always critical then this will simply reinforce a child's negative view of himself.

Unfortunately, humans are a bit like news reporters. We tend only to report the bad things in the world. Thus we usually remind children that they are 'naughty' or 'bad', and we forget about the good things they have done. Remembering to praise children even for the slightest positive thing may have an enormous positive effect on the child. For example, if Daniel missed the penalty kick in the soccer match and the team lost the cup, at least Daniel deserves praise for helping his team get to the final and being chosen for the team. Obviously this is not going to immediately take away the pain of losing the cup, but that little bit of praise, however small, is still priceless in terms of shaping Daniel's confidence.

Remember to make sure the praise is not false or children will see straight through you. For example, do not say 'Well done, you are a star!' if your child got one out of ten in spelling. Praise for trying at spelling is OK if you felt your child was at least trying and should be followed with gentle encouragement and an exploration of ways you can help him improve on that spelling score.

At the same time one has to get the balance right with boundaries and limits as one does not want to create arrogant children. So the message is: praise whenever you can but do so with good sense and limits.

Support and encouragement

In order to get a child to try things, he needs to feel that his parents support him no matter what happens. Parents should give lots of praise when their child achieves things but, equally, when something does not work out, the child needs to know that mum and dad do not think any worse of him. Be encouraging with comments like 'Not to worry, you did your best' and 'Well done for giving it a go, I'm proud of you'. Showing faith in your child's ideas and abilities is important for his self-belief. The child who is willing to try and knows he will not be judged if he fails is a child with confidence who can handle most of the challenges life throws at him.

Give your child responsibility

Responsibility may involve everyday things such as 'cleaning out the goldfish bowl once a month' and 'helping dad cut the hedges in the garden'. This should be balanced with responsibility for fun things such as helping to choose 'what present to take to Uncle Joe's birthday party' or 'deciding on what takeaway the family eat on Friday night'. By giving the child little tasks, such as laying the table or pouring the drinks, it shows that you are expecting some degree of competence from him. As he contributes more to family life he will feel better about himself.

Responsibility in school is also helpful for building up self-esteem. This can be something simple: being in charge of the pencils and making sure they are sharpened or choosing what story should be read by the class out of a selection. Unfortunately the child with tics and Tourette Syndrome is often passed over by teachers when it comes to handing out tasks and duties. This may be due to the fact that the teacher thinks the child with tics is incapable of simple tasks and is likely to have a detrimental effect on a child's self-esteem. Many adults with Tourette Syndrome recall not being asked to take part in reading out aloud in class or not given lead parts on stage in school productions. In fact many people with Tourette

Syndrome may be relieved and grateful to avoid the spotlight but equally there are many who would at least like to have been given the opportunity of playing the leading role.

Laugh and enjoy things together

Yes, the old cliché 'laughter is the best medicine' is true. Humour is an important way of making us feel good about ourselves. It is very good for dealing with stress and is a way of coping with life's obstacles. Doing things with parents or as a family unit is also important. It gives a child a sense of comfort and belonging. Most children get pleasure and satisfaction if their parents have also been able to take part in fun things with them, such as day trips, going for a meal or simply watching TV together. As your child grows up, he will have pleasant memories of his childhood to look back on and will feel good about himself.

Give them lots of experiences

Help your child find things that inspire and excite him by giving him the opportunity to experience a variety of things. This may be through going to museums, cinemas, theatres, libraries and scout groups. Encourage him to take up hobbies and join clubs. These activities do not need to be expensive, as often there are discounts for certain activities and free days for exhibitions.

Sports are useful for children with Tourette Syndrome as they may help with their coordination; they are also an outlet to release physical energy. If the child is able to excel in the sport then this is a bonus.

Going to a football stadium is a good place to watch sports since it is noisy and exciting. Most of the audience will be too preoccupied to notice any vocal or motor tics in children.

Team sports such as football and hockey encourage teamwork and provide children with good social support. Martial arts lessons may be helpful not only in teaching the child to protect himself from bullies, but also as a valuable way of teaching discipline and channelling aggression.

Playing a musical instrument can be relaxing and rewarding. There are many successful musicians with tics.

Enhance your child's strengths

The problem with school is that we have to do a bit of everything, from maths and English to languages, science and physical education. We cannot be good at all subjects and most of us drop the subjects we dislike as soon as we can. We usually choose careers that involve something that we are good at. We definitely avoid career choices that involve things we are bad at. Hence if you child is only good at one subject at school, still praise him for that and perhaps exploit that strength. For instance, if Sanjay is only good at working with computers then by all means help him with other subjects but remember to encourage his passion for computers. With the right amount of praise, a job with a computer firm may be his future.

Strengths do not just apply to school work. Praising your child for other strengths such as caring for his pet or getting along with his friends is invaluable for his self-esteem and encourages your child to feel good about himself. It also stops him thinking about negative things in his life. Too often we focus on the things we cannot do rather than the things we *can* do. If your child only sees himself as someone with Tourette Syndrome and nothing else, help him to see the other characteristics and qualities he possesses. He may be helped if you get him to write a list of the positive things about himself or his life.

Teach your child to cope with disappointment

Things don't always go our way so it's important that we learn to cope with disappointment. Help your child cope by acknowledging how he must be feeling when things go wrong and praising him for trying. Give him lots of hugs and attention. It may be helpful to tell him how you felt disappointed in a similar situation in your childhood but that something good came out of it in the end.

Coping with disappointment is important for developing social skills and building friendships. Many parents of children with Tourette Syndrome often describe their child as being highly competitive and needing to win every time he plays a board game or game of cards. This leads on to arguments and eventually his friends start to avoid him. Learning to accept defeat gracefully can improve peer relationships.

Stay calm and relaxed

If a parent is calm and relaxed then this will make the child feel safe and contained. If the child can learn to relax and unwind then this may also help his self-esteem. As mentioned earlier in Chapter 6, relaxation is helpful not only for tics but also for anger management. One also forgets that children look to parents as role models. If the parent is always critical or pessimistic about things then the child is likely to grow up having similar traits.

Actively listen to your child

Let your child know that you are actually listening to him even when he is arguing or complaining. Repeating things back to him to clarify what he has said is often a good way of letting him know that you have heard him. It also prevents any misunderstanding. Use non-judgemental questions when your child has done something that may meet with disapproval. For example, avoid saying 'Why did you do that?' and instead say 'What made you do that?' Be sympathetic and reflect feelings, saying things such as 'That must feel frustrating' or 'I'm not surprised you feel angry'. Again, this shows that you are listening to your child and he is more likely to respect you for this.

Be generous with love and affection

Show your child you love him by giving old-fashioned hugs and kisses. If your child is someone who squirms at kisses and cuddles, let him know you appreciate him by telling them directly that you enjoy his company. Let your child see you demonstrating love and affection for key people in your life such as partners and relatives. This allows your child to express affection to others, which will also enhance his own self-esteem in the long term.

Glossary

Akathisia

Increased restlessness. May be side-effects of *neuroleptic* medication.

Arrhythmia

Abnormal rhythm of the heart.

Athetosis

Slow, sinuous, writhing movements performed involuntary and especially severe in the hands.

Attention Deficit Hyperactivity Disorder

A developmental disorder involving difficulties with attention, impulsivity and hyperactivity.

Autistic spectrum disorder

A neurodevelopmental disorder with core symptoms such as social skills deficits, problems with communication and the need for rituals and routines.

Chorea

Involuntary, abrupt, irregular and random movements. Can be large amplitude movements.

Coprolalia

Repetitive use of obscene or socially unacceptable words or phrases.

Copropraxia

Making obscene gestures.

Creutzfeldt-Jakob Disease

A rare form of infection in the brain caused by a virus termed a prion.

Dopamine

A *neurotransmitter* involved in *Tourette Syndrome* and other movement disorders.

Down Syndrome

A congenital disorder where a person is born with three copies of Chromosome 21. Signs and symptoms include mental retardation, broad hands, short fingers, slanting eyes and a broad, short skull.

Dystonia

A sustained muscle contraction leading to repetitive movements or abnormal postures.

Echolalia

Repeating other people's words.

Echopraxia

Imitation of gestures or movements of others.

Fragile X

A condition in which a child or adult has features of large ears, long face, large testes and, usually, mental retardation.

Huntington's Disease

A progressive genetic disorder that begins in young to middle age, consists of writhing movements of the arms and obsessional features, and leads to dementia.

Klinefelter's Syndrome

A chromosomal disorder in which males have an extra X (female) chromosome. They are usually tall and feminine in appearance.

Myoclonus

Spasm of a muscle or group of muscles.

Neuroleptic

A classification of drugs also known as major tranquillizers. It includes haloperidol and risperidone.

Neurosyphilis

An advanced syphilis infection in adults that affects the nervous system. Symptoms include unsteady gait, dementia and balancing difficulties.

Neurotransmitter

A chemical carrying nerve impulses across a synapse (see *pre-synaptic receptor* below).

Obsessive Compulsive Disorder

A disorder involving recurrent, intrusive thoughts, known as obsessions, and the need to perform certain habits and routines, known as compulsions.

Palilalia

Repeating one's own words.

Premonitory urge

A sensation immediately preceding a motor or vocal *tic*.

Pre-synaptic receptor

A synapse is the gap between nerve endings. *Neurotransmitters* are transported across this gap. There are two types of receptors at the nerve endings. The pre-synaptic receptor is the site where neurotransmitters are sent from. The neurotransmitters are then received at the post-synaptic receptors.

Schizophrenia

A mental health disorder mainly affecting older adolescents and adults. Symptoms include auditory hallucinations, thought disorder, delusions and deterioration in functioning.

Serotonin

A *neurotransmitter* involved in *Obsessive Compulsive Disorder* and depression.

Special educational needs coordinator

A teacher who is responsible for children with special educational needs.

Statement

A legal document that sets out a child's educational needs and all the special help to which he should be entitled to.

Sydenham's Chorea

A post-infectious chorea that appears several months after a streptococcal infection with subsequent rheumatic fever occurs. The chorea typically involves distal limbs and is associated with hypotonia and emotional lability. Improvement occurs over weeks or months.

Tics

Involuntary, rapid, recurrent, non-rhythmic motor or vocal actions.

Tourette Syndrome

A condition involving motor and vocal *tics*.

Tuberous sclerosis

A genetic disorder with symptoms that include seizures, retardation and skin lesions.

Waxing and waning

The naturally occurring increases and decreases of severity and frequency of *tics*.

Wilson's Disease

An inherited disorder where there is an excess of copper in tissues such as the liver and nervous system.

APPENDIX II

Useful Reading Material and Addresses

Further reading

Carroll, A. and Robertson, M.M. (2000) *Tourette Syndrome: A Practical Guide for Teachers, Parents and Carers*. London: David Fulton Publishers. ISBN 1-85346-656-5.

Elliott, M. (1997) *101 Ways to Deal with Bullying: A Guide for Parents*. London: Hodder and Stoughton. ISBN 0-340-69519-6.

Greene, R.W. (2001) *The Explosive Child*. New York: HarperCollins. ISBN 0-06-093102-7.

Phelan, T.W. (1995) *1-2-3 Magic: Effective Discipline for Children 2–12*. Glen Ellyn, IL: Child Management Inc. ISBN 0-9633861-9-0.

Support networks

Tourette Syndrome Association (UK)
PO Box 26149
Dunfermline KY12 7YU
www.tsa.org.uk

Tourette Syndrome Foundation of Canada
206–194 Jarvis Street
Toronto
Ontario M5B 2B7
www.tourette.ca

Tourette Syndrome Association (US)
42–40 Bell Boulevard
Bayside
New York 11631-2820
www.tsa.mgh.harvard.edu

ADD Information Services (UK)
PO Box 340
Edgware
Middlesex HA8 9HL
www.addiss.co.uk

CHADD Canada Inc.
1376 Bank Street
Ottawa
Ontario K1H 7Y3
www.chaddcanada.org

CHADD (US)
8181 Professional Place
Suite 150
Landover
MD 20785
www.chadd.org

OCD Action (UK)
Aberdeen Centre
22–24 Highbury Grove
London N5 2EA
www.ocdaction.org.uk

Obsessive-Compulsive Foundation (OCF) (US)
676 State Street
New Haven
CT 06511
www.ocfoundation.org

References

American Academy of Child and Adolescent Psychiatry (1998) 'Practice Parameters for the Assessment and Treatment of Children and Adolescents with Obsessive-Compulsive Disorder.' *Journal of the American Academy of Child and Adolescent Psychiatry 37* (10 Supplement), 27–45.

American Psychiatric Association (1994) *Diagnostic and Statistical Manual of Mental Disorders, Fourth Edition* (DSM-IV). Washington DC: American Psychiatric Association.

Azrin, N.H. and Nunn, R.G. (1973) 'A method of eliminating nervous habits and tics.' *Behaviour Research and Therapy 11*, 619–28.

Baron-Cohen, S., Mortimore, C., Moriarty, J., Izaguirre, J. and Robertson, M. (1999) 'The prevalence of Gilles de la Tourette's Syndrome in children and adolescents with autism.' *Journal of Child Psychology and Psychiatry 40*, 2, 213–18.

Barrett, P., Healey-Famel, L. and March, J.S. (2004) 'Cognitive-behavioural family treatment of childhood Obsessive Compulsive Disorder: A controlled trial.' *Journal of the American Academy of Child and Adolescent Psychiatry 43*, 1, 46–62.

Berg, C.J., Rapoport, J.L. and Flament, M. (1986) 'The Leyton Obsessionality Inventory–Child Version.' *Journal of the American Academy of Child and Adolescent Psychiatry 25*, 84–91.

British National Formulary (2003) BNF, March 2003. London: British Medical Association and Royal Pharmaceutical Society of Great Britain.

Budman, C., Brunn, R., Park, K., Lesser, M. and Olson, M. (2000) 'Explosive outbursts in children with Tourette's disorder.' *Journal of the American Academy of Child and Adolescent Psychiatry 39*, 1270–6.

Burd, L., Kerbeshian, P.J, Barth, A., Klug, M., Avery, P. and Benz, B. (2001) 'Long term follow-up of an epidemiologically defined cohort of patients with Tourette syndrome.' *Journal of Child Neurology 16*, 431–7.

Chambless, D.L. and Steketee, G. (1999) 'Expressed emotion and behaviour therapy outcome: A prospective study with obsessive-compulsive and agoraphobic patients.' *Journal of Consulting and Clinical Psychology 67,* 658–65.

Comings, D.E. and Comings, B.G. (1987) 'A controlled study of Tourette Syndrome, I–VII.' *American Journal of Human Genetics 41,* 701–866.

Conners, C.K. (1997) *Connors Rating Scales–Revised.* Windsor, UK: NFER.

Dale, R.C., Church, A.J., Surtees, R.A., Thompson, E.J., Giovannoni, G. and Neville, B.G. (2002) 'Post streptococcal autoimmune neuropsychiatric disease presenting as paroxysmal dystonic choreoathetosis.' *Movement Disorders 17,* 817–20.

Demirkiran, M. and Jankovic, J. (1995) 'Paroxysmal dyskinesias: Clinical features and classification.' *Annals of Neurology 38,* 571–9.

Department for Education (1994) *Special Educational Needs – A Guide for Parents.* London: HMSO.

DiFazio, M.P., Morales, J. and Davis, R. (1998) 'Acute myoclonus secondary to Group A beta-hemolytic streptococcus infection: A PANDAS variant.' *Journal of Child Neurology 13,* 616–18.

Dulcan, M. (1997) 'Practice parameters for the assessment of children, adolescents, and adults with attention deficit/hyperactivity disorder.' *Journal of American Academy of Child and Adolescent Psychiatry 36* (supplement), 85–121.

Eapen, V., Pauls, D.L. and Robertson, M.M. (1993) 'Evidence for autosomal dominant transmission in Tourette syndrome: United Kingdom cohort study.' *British Journal of Psychiatry 162,* 593–6.

Eapen, V., Robertson, M.M., Zeitlin, H. and Kurlan, R. (1997) 'Gilles de la Tourette's Syndrome in special education schools: A United Kingdom study.' *Journal of Neurology 244,* 378–82.

Evers, R.A.F. and van de Wetering, B.J.M. (1994) 'A treatment model for motor tics based on a specific tension reduction technique.' *Journal of Behavioural Therapy and Experimental Psychiatry 25,* 3, 255–60.

Gaffney, G.R., Sieg, K. and Hellings, J. (1994) 'The MOVES: A self-rating scale for Tourette's Syndrome.' *Journal of Child and Adolescent Psychopharmacology 44,* 4, 269–80.

Geller, D., Biederman, J., Jones, J., Park, K., Schwartz, S., Shapiro, S. and Coffey, C. (1998) 'Is Juvenile OCD a developmental subtype of the disorder? A review of the paediatric literature.' *Journal of the American Academy of Child and Adolescent Psychiatry 37,* 4, 420–7.

George, M.S., Trimble, M.R., Ring, H.A., Sallee, F.R. and Robertson, M.M. (1993) 'Obsessions in Obsessive-Compulsive Disorder with and without Gilles de la Tourette's Syndrome.' *American Journal of Psychiatry 150,* 93–7.

Gerard, E. and Peterson, B.S. (2003) 'Developmental processes and brain imaging studies in Tourette Syndrome.' *Journal of Psychosomatic Research 55*, 13–22.

Giedd, J.N., Rapoport, J.L., Garvey, M.A., Perlmutter, S. and Swedo, S.E. (2000) 'MRI assessment of children with Obsessive Compulsive Disorder or tics associated with streptococcal infections.' *Biological Psychiatry 45*, 1564–71.

Hall, M., Costa, D.C. and Shields, J. (1990) 'Brain perfusion patterns with Tc-99m-HMPAO/SPET in patients with Gilles de la Tourette Syndrome.' *European Journal of Nuclear Medicine 16*, 18.

Heyman, I., Fombonne, E., Simmons, H., Meltzer, H. and Goodman, R. (2001) 'Prevalence of Obsessive Compulsive Disorder in the British nationwide survey of child mental health.' *British Journal of Psychiatry 179*, 324–9.

Hill, P. and Cameron, M. (1999) 'Recognising hyperactivity: A guide for the cautious clinician.' *Child Psychology and Psychiatry Review 4*, 2, 50–60.

Holzer, J., Goodman, W.K., Price, L.H., Bear, L., Leckman, J.F. and Heninger, G.R. (1994) 'Obsessive compulsive disorder with and without a chronic tic disorder: A comparison of symptoms in 70 patients.' *British Journal of Psychiatry 164*, 469–73.

Hornsey, H., Banerjee, S., Zeitlin, H. and Robertson, M.M. (2001) 'The prevalence of Tourette Syndrome in 13–14-year-olds in mainstream schools.' *Journal of Child Psychology and Psychiatry 42*, 8, 1035–9.

Hyde, T.M., Aaronson, B.A., Randolph, C., Rickler, K.C. and Weinberger, D.R. (1992) 'Relationship of birth weight to the phenotypic expression of Gilles de la Tourette Syndrome in monozygotic twins.' *Neurology 42*, 652–8.

Kadesjo, B. and Gillberg, C. (2000) 'Tourette's disorder: Epidemiology and comorbidity in primary school children.' *Journal of American Academy of Child and Adolescent Psychiatry 39*, 5, 548–55.

Kostanecka-Endress, T., Banaschewski, T., Kinkelbur, J., Wullner, I., Lichtblau, S., Cohrs, S., Ruther, E., Woerner, W., Hajak, G. and Rothenberger, A. (2003) 'Disturbed sleep in children with Tourette Syndrome: A polysomnographic study.' *Journal of Psychosomatic Research 55*, 23–9.

Kumar, R. and Lang, A.E. (1997) 'Tourette Syndrome: Secondary tic disorders [review].' *Neurology Clinics 15*, 309–31.

Leckman, J.F., Price, R.A., Walkup, J.T., Ort, S., Pauls, D.L. and Cohen, D.J. (1987) 'Nongenetic factors in Gilles de la Tourette's Syndrome [letter].' *Archives of General Psychiatry 44*, 100.

Leckman, J.F., Riddle, M.A., Hardin, M., Ort, S., Swartz, K.L., Stevenson, J. and Cohen, D.J. (1989) 'The Yale Global Tic Severity Scale: Initial testing of a clinician-rated scale of tic severity.' *Journal of the American Academy of Child and Adolescent Psychiatry 28*, 4, 566–73.

Leckman, J.F., Dolnansky, E.S., Hardin, M.T., Clubb, M., Walkup, J.T., Stevenson, J. and Pauls, D.L. (1990) 'Perinatal factors in the expression of Tourette's syndrome: An exploratory study.' *Journal of the American Academy of Child and Adolescent Psychiatry 29*, 220–6.

Leckman, J.F., Walker, D.E., Goodman, W.K., Pauls, D.L. and Cohen, D.J. (1994) '"Just right" perceptions associated with compulsive behaviour in Tourette Syndrome.' *American Journal of Psychiatry 151*, 675–80.

Leckman, J.F., Grice, D.E., Barr, L., de Vries, A.L.C., Martin, C., Cohen, D.J., McDougle, C.J., Goodman, W.K. and Rasmussen, S. (1994/1995) 'Tic-related vs. non-tic-related Obsessive Compulsive Disorder.' *Anxiety 1*, 208–15.

Leckman, J.F., Zhang, H., Vitale, A., Lahnin, F., Lynch, K., Bondi, C., Kim, Y.S. and Peterson, B.S. (1998) 'Course of tic severity in Tourette Syndrome: The first two decades.' *Pediatrics 102*, 14–19.

Leckman, J.F., Cohen, D.J., Getz, C.G. and Jankovic, J. (2001) 'Tourette Syndrome: Pieces of the puzzle.' *Advances in Neurology 85*, 369–90.

March, J.S. and Mulle, K. (1998) *OCD in Children and Adolescents: A Cognitive-Behavioural Treatment Manual.* New York: Guilford Press.

Moriarty, J., Costa, D.C., Schmitz, B., Trimble, M.R., Ell, P.J. and Robertson, M.M. (1995) 'Brain perfusion abnormalities in Gilles de la Tourette's syndrome.' *British Journal of Psychiatry 167*, 249–54.

The MTA Cooperative Group (1999) 'A 14-month randomised clinical trial of treatment strategies for attention-deficit/hyperactivity disorder.' *Archives of General Psychiatry 56*, 1073–86.

NICE (National Institute for Clinical Excellence) (2000) *Guidance for the Use of Methylphenidate for Attention Deficit Hyperactivity Disorder (ADHD) in Childhood.* London: NICE.

O'Connor, K.P. and Gareau, D. (1994) *Tics et Problemes de Tension Musculaire.* Quebec, Canada: Sogides.

Olweus, D. (1994) 'Annotation: Bullying at school. Basic facts and effects of a school based intervention program.' *Journal of Child Psychology and Psychiatry 35*, 7, 1171–90.

Peterson, B.S. and Cohen, D.J. (1998) 'The treatment of Tourette Syndrome: Multimodal, developmental intervention.' *Journal of Clinical Psychiatry 59*, 62–72.

Peterson, B. and Thomas, P. (2000) 'Tourette's Syndrome: What are we really imaging?' In M. Ernst and J. Rumsey (eds) *Functional Neuroimaging in Child Psychiatry*. Cambridge, UK: Cambridge University Press.

Peterson, B.S., Staib, L., Scahill, L., Zhang, H., Anderson, C., Leckman, J.F., Cohen, D.J., Gore, J.C., Albert, J. and Webster, R. (2001) 'Regional brain and ventricular volumes in Tourette syndrome.' *Archives of General Psychiatry 58*, 427–40.

Phelan, T.W. (1995) *1-2-3 Magic: Effective Discipline for Children 2–12*. Glen Ellyn, IL: Child Management Inc.

Robertson, M.M. (1994) 'Annotation: Gilles de la Tourette's syndrome – an update [review].' *Journal of Child Psychology and Psychiatry 35*, 597–611.

Robertson, M.M. (2000) 'Invited review: Tourette Syndrome, associated conditions and the complexities of treatment.' *Brain 123*, 425–62.

Robertson, M.M. and Eapen, V. (1996) 'The National Hospital Interview Schedule for the assessment of Gilles de la Tourette Syndrome.' *International Journal of Methods in Psychiatric Research 6*, 203–26.

Robertson M.M., Banerjee, S., Hiley, P.J. and Tannock, C. (1997) 'Personality disorder and psychopathology in Tourette's Syndrome: A controlled study.' *British Journal of Psychiatry 171*, 283–6.

Rothenberger, A., Kostanecka, T., Kinkelbur, J., Cohrs, S., Woerner, W. and Hajak, G. (2001) 'Sleep and Tourette Syndrome.' *Advances in Neurology 85*, 245–59.

Scahill, L., Riddle, M.A., McSwiggin-Hardin, M., Ort, S.I., King, R.A., Goodman, W., Cicchetti, D. and Leckman, J. (1997) 'Children's Yale-Brown Obsessive Compulsive Scale: Reliability and validity.' *Journal of the American Academy of Child and Adolescent Psychiatry 36*, 844–52.

Simonoff, E., Elander, J., Holmshaw, J., Pickles, A., Murray, R. and Rutter, M. (2004) 'Predictors of antisocial personality: Continuities from childhood to adult life.' *British Journal of Psychiatry 184*, 118–27.

Singer, H. (2000) 'Current issues in Tourette's Syndrome.' *Movement Disorders 15*, 1051–63.

Singer, H.S., Giuliano, J.D., Hansen, B.H., Hallett, J.J., Laurino, J.P., Benson, M. and Kiessling, L.S. (1999) 'Antibodies against a neuron-like (HTB-10 neuroblastoma) cell in children with Tourette Syndrome.' *Biological Psychiatry 46*, 775–80.

Sokol, M.S. (2000) 'Infection-triggered anorexia nervosa in children: Clinical description of four cases.' *Journal of Child and Adolescent Psychopharmacology 10*, 133–45.

Swedo, S.E., Leonard, H.L., Garvey, M., Mittleman, B.B., Allen, A.J., Perlmutter, S., Dow, S.P., Zamkoff, J., Dubbert, B.K. and Lougee, L. (1998) 'Pediatric autoimmune neuropsychiatric disorders associated with streptococcal infections: Clinical description of the first 50 cases.' *American Journal of Psychiatry 155*, 264–71.

Taylor, E., Sergeant, J., Doepfner, M., Gunning, B., Overmeyer, S., Mobius, H-J. and Eisert, H-G. (1998) 'Clinical guidelines for Hyperkinetic Disorder.' *European Child and Adolescent Psychiatry 7*, 184–200.

The Tourette Syndrome Classification Study Group (1993) 'Definitions and classification of tic disorders.' *Archives of Neurology 50*, 1013–16.

Wand, R., Matazow, G., Shady, G., Furer, P. and Staley, D. (1993) 'Tourette Syndrome: Associated symptoms and most disabling features.' *Neuroscience and Biobehavioural Review 17*, 271–5.

Waters, T.L., Barrett, P.M. and March, J.S. (2001) 'Cognitive-behavioural family treatment of childhood obsessive-compulsive disorder.' *American Journal of Psychotherapy 55*, 3, 372–87.

Wodrich, D.L., Benjamin, E. and Lachar, D. (1997) 'Tourette's Syndrome and psychopathology in a child psychiatry setting.' *Journal of the American Academy of Child and Adolescent Psychiatry 36*, 1, 1618–24.

Wolf, S.S., Jones, D.W., Knable, M.B., Gorey, J.G., Lee, K.S., Hyde, T.M., Coppola, R. and Weinberger, D.R. (1996) 'Tourette Syndrome: Prediction of phenotypic variation in monozygotic twins by caudate nucleus D2 receptor binding.' *Science 273*, 1225–7.

World Health Organization (1992) *The Tenth Revision of the International Classification of Diseases and Related Health Problems* (ICD-10). Geneva: WHO.

Subject Index

Author
Index